Also on YouTube

BEHOLD
UNCOVERING YOUR IDENTITY IN CHRIST
by Sher Pai

ISBN 978-0-9961006-6-3
Copyright © 2018 by Sher Pai

Published by Flying Arrow Ministries
www.flyingarrowministries.com

No part of this book may be reproduced in any written, electronic, recording, or photocopying form without the prior permission of the author, Sher Pai.

Unless otherwise noted, all Scripture quotations are taken from the New King James Version®. Copyright © 1982 by Thomas Nelson, Inc. Used by permission. All rights reserved. Scripture quotations marked (NIV) are taken from The Holy Bible, New International Version®, Copyright © 1973, 1978, 1984, 2011 by Biblica, Inc.® Used by permission. All rights reserved worldwide. Scripture quotations marked (NLT) are taken from the Holy Bible, New Living Translation, copyright © 1996, 2004, 2007 by Tyndale House Foundation. Used by permission of Tyndale House Publishers, Inc., Carol Stream, Illinois 60188. All rights reserved. Scripture quotations marked (HCSB) are taken from the Holman Christian Standard Bible®, Copyright © 1999, 2000, 2002, 2003 by Holman Bible Publishers. Used by permission. Holman Christian Standard Bible®, Holman CSB®, and HCSB® are federally registered trademarks of Holman Bible Publishers. Scripture quotations marked (ESV) are from The ESV® Bible (The Holy Bible, English Standard Version®), copyright © 2001 by Crossway, a publishing ministry of Good News Publishers. Used by permission. All rights reserved. The Holy Bible, Berean Study Bible, BSB Copyright ©2016, 2018 by Bible Hub Used by Permission. All Rights Reserved Worldwide.

Editor, internal & cover layout: Juleen Lak

Cover art: Sher Pai

Internal art sketches: Sher Pai & Heather Danielle Stevens

BEHOLD
UNCOVERING YOUR IDENTITY IN CHRIST

SHER PAI

FLYING ARROW
ministries
FLYINGARROWMINISTRIES.COM

CONTENTS

Introduction	NOT MAN MADE	6
	WHO IN THE WORLD AM I?	8
	BEHOLD	12
Chapter 1.	MADE BY GOD	15
Chapter 2.	JESUS IDENTIFIED	25
Chapter 3.	I AM IN CHRIST	33
Chapter 4.	I AM ACCEPTED	43
Chapter 5.	I AM JUSTIFIED	55
Chapter 6.	I AM GOD'S CHILD	63
Chapter 7.	I AM A NEW CREATURE	73
Chapter 8.	I AM COMPLETE	87
Chapter 9.	I AM SECURE	97
Chapter 10.	I AM ROOTED	105
Chapter 11.	I AM MORE THAN A CONQUEROR	117
Chapter 12.	I AM SIGNIFICANT	127
Chapter 13.	I AM A MASTERPIECE	135
Chapter 14.	I AM A FRUIT BEARER	145
Chapter 15.	I AM AN AMBASSADOR	159
Chapter 16.	IDENTIFIED	169

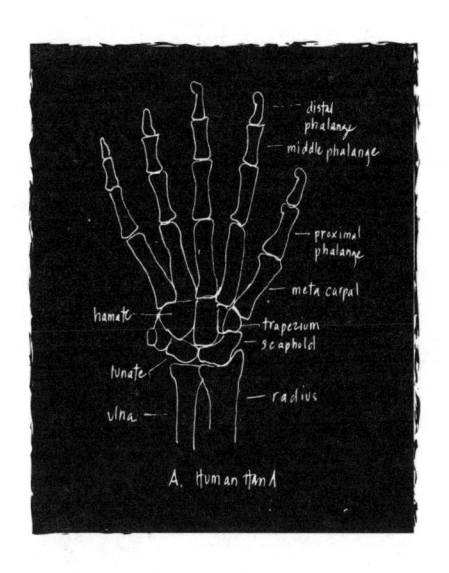

INTRODUCTION

NOT MAN MADE

WHO IN THE WORLD AM I?

BEHOLD

NOT MAN MADE

I can't ignore the irony, as I lay here in my bed writing, my face is scabbed over and swollen, only slightly recognizable. I am hiding out from the sun and from my grandkids so that I don't frighten them. I need to stay focused on the purpose of this painful process, which is to eradicate harmful, pre-cancerous skin cells. When the treatment is finished I will have new and healthy skin cells. But in the meantime, I am feeling the destruction, havoc, pain and burning. I definitely look like a restoration project. I keep reminding myself that this is only temporary, the pain will go away, it's going to be worth it. I find myself thankful for the reminders from God that I am just a pilgrim here on earth, just passing through, my tent is my body and I am on my way Home. Health, beauty, strength, prosperity, poverty—they come and go and then they are gone. The fade, the flab, the crinkles, the pain are temporary too. Soon, very soon we will see Jesus face to face.

God has His ways of shaking us up and shaking us down! He faithfully allows the temporal props we are prone to lean on to crumble under us. We attempt to take from the material world and try to fashion for ourselves an identity, but God won't allow it. Satan whispers lies diminishing our value, speaking enough truth to get our attention causing us to doubt the love, power and plans of God for our lives. Without our identity firmly rooted and grounded in Him we will carefully craft and project an image for ourselves.

When careless words from parents, siblings, teachers, peers and coaches are spoken over our lives they can leave impressions upon our souls. When left untouched by the redeeming power of Jesus those words can cast a life into a statue-like form, trapped and frozen, stuck in an image shaped by others. We are soft and vulnerable beings whether we like to admit it or not, susceptible to the influence of the world.

Every soul craves to belong, to be loved, accepted, and to have purpose. To attempt to find these things fulfilled and answered apart from God usually have painful and destructive results.

It has been alarming to see the Christian community just as plagued and ravaged by the effects of not knowing who we are in Christ as those who don't belong to God. The results are seen in every part of God's body: men, women, children, elderly, rich, poor, healthy and sick. Not believing who we are in Jesus Christ leaves us corporately and individually weak, distracted, unstable, insecure and susceptible to allowing something and someone other than God to shape and define an identity for us.

Understanding who we are in Christ is not an end in itself. It is the means to the end of self-focus, self-confidence and self-esteem. It is a means to freedom from chronic preoccupation with self, releasing us to live in a healthy and thriving right relationship with God, with others, even with nature—in peace, joy, stability, power and significance.

The purpose of this book is to not only bring shape and purpose as to your identity in Christ through what is clearly defined in Scripture but to challenge you to honestly examine your belief in those truths. Therein lies the victory of the matter—believing you are who God says you are and who Christ died for you to be.

WHO IN THE WORLD AM I?

A few summers ago a young woman I had been mentoring was getting ready to move away to attend college. She asked if we could use our remaining time together to learn about her identity in Christ. She was starting to make the connection between her insecurities and her behavior and felt they were somehow tied to her faith. I was excited by the challenge. As I started to investigate what God's Word says about who we are in Christ, I was surprised by the amount of information and detail given in the Bible. Each truth was like the brush stroke of a painting bringing greater definition, illumination, form and function to the image of man. God's Word clearly describes us as a new creation in Christ, and it's a picture of grace, of a people who are lovingly accepted, cherished, securely kept and significant in God's plans and purpose.

Week by week we looked deeply into who God says we are. I soon realized that understanding our identity in Christ is powerful knowledge—with the potential to change the way we not only see ourselves but also the way we perceive and relate to God, people and nature. As our study progressed we began to feel the real challenge of these discoveries: Do I believe I am who God says I am?

This was a question that required an honest examination and needed to be settled. Until we believe we are all God says we are in Christ we will be vulnerable to the forces of the world, Satan, others and even ourselves to define, shape and mold an identity for us.

Who am I and why am I here are curiosities that are hard-wired into humanity. Questions about our identity are not isolated to gender, age or culture. Our identity will never fully take shape until we look fully upon Jesus. To find Christ and to know Him is to find the truth of who we really are. Man was created in God's image, and the Spirit of God is at work recreating and renewing us into the image of Christ.

I recently read an article informing about a resource developed to help explain and describe gender identity to school children. A purple unicorn cartoon character is used to help the children identify their gender male/female/other by determining if they are sexually attracted to male/female/other gender(s), romantically attracted to male/female/other gender(s), and questions their gender expression/presentation male/female/other.

We can't choose our gender! And we don't choose our identity, but we can choose what and who we allow to inform us concerning our identity. Every baby ever conceived has been shaped and created by God, in His image. God assigns gender. And God's Word is the only resource we should trust to inform us about our identity. Expressions of our identity are manifest through our behavior. Our behavior is a reflection of our belief in who we think we are.

Until our faith is firmly wrapped and rooted into the fibers of the truth of our identity in Christ, we will be unstable, insecure and constantly impressed, depressed and misshapen by the world, Satan, our pride and our fears. We must know the truth and choose to believe it. We must allow God to work in the deepest places of our soul to both heal and to make whole, to believe the truth and reject the lies. You may be thinking, "You don't know what I have been through, you don't understand the rejection, neglect and abuse I have received from the hands of man." I may not know, but Satan has seen it, and he is exploiting it for all its worth. But greater still is the fact that God has seen and heard and He sent His Son to redeem, restore and reveal to you your true identity in

Christ: you are loved, accepted, secured, made new and full of purpose.

This Bible study is meant to challenge you to not just know who you are but to believe who you are in Christ. I am thankful for that summer that God brought the challenge to go deeper, to be honest with myself and with Him, to allow Him to test the genuineness of my faith in these truths of my identity. Not that knowing our identity is the end all, but that in knowing and trusting we are who God says we are in Christ, we can now live and relate freely—free from self-focus, free to serve God with joy, free to love others with abandon and to care for nature as God intended.

Satan teaches men first to doubt and then to deny; he makes them skeptics first, and so by degrees makes them atheists.
Matthew Henry

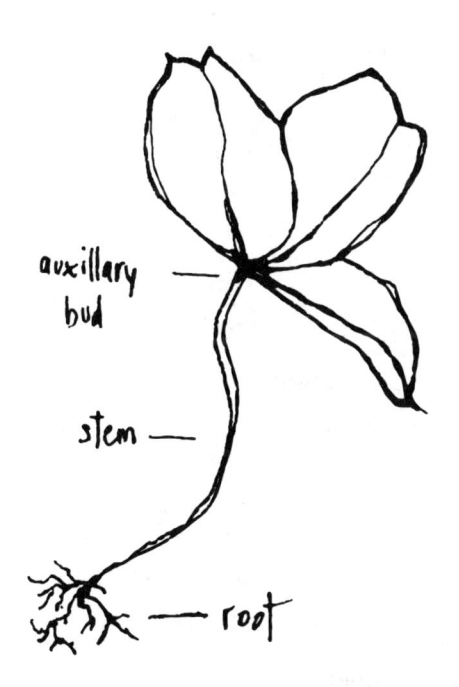

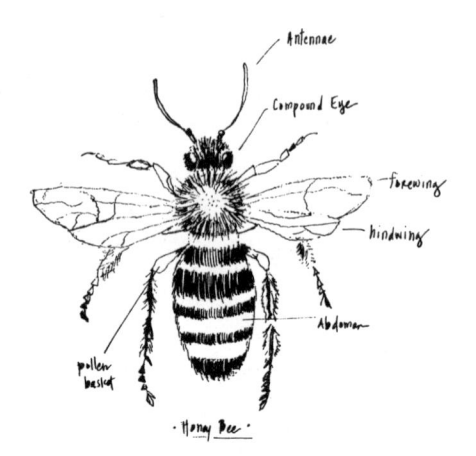

BEHOLD

BEHOLD...what you are about to read may seem impossible and yet has happened!

The word *behold* is used by the Holy Spirit from Genesis to Revelation like a teacher shaking us out of our sleepy listening. It is strategically placed in the Bible to quicken us, waking us up before we read on. When we see this vivacious word, it should grab our attention. What we will be told after the behold is something unexpected and yet sure! It is meant to excite and perk us up to what is about to be communicated.

The purpose of this study is to not only inform but to challenge your belief in your identity in Christ.

May God's Spirit awaken you as you read and study, may He quicken your faith to believe that what you are reading, though seemingly impossible at times, is true.

At the end of each chapter is an opportunity for you to respond to what was uncovered about your identity through your time in God's Word by BEHOLDING its truths.

Believe it!
Was something uncovered about your identity in this chapter that is challenging your faith?

Enjoy it!
What did you behold about your identity in this chapter that has you excited?

Honor it!
Make a decision to honor God by choosing to believe what He says about who you are in Christ. Write your declaration: (i.e., I choose to honor Your Word, God, by believing You have made me a new creation in Christ.)

Observe it!
Hear and attend to what you learned from this chapter. Take a closer look, thoroughly examine what the Bible uncovers about God's ability, plans and purpose, Jesus' nature, or your identity. Do a word study, a character study. Is there more to uncover? Get curious!

Live it!
Choose to conform to your new identity by living it out.

Depend on it!
Is there anything that was uncovered in this chapter that seems impossible and yet is promised? Write out the promise and memorize it.

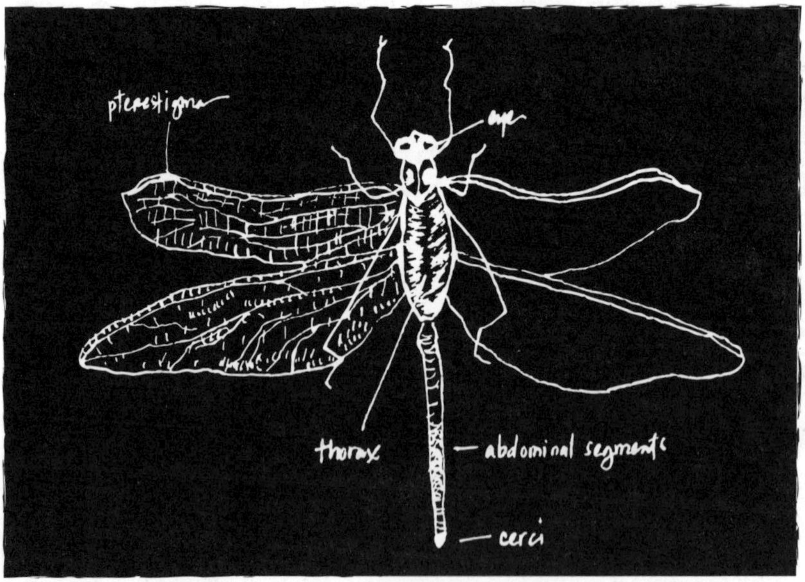
pterostigma
eye
thorax
abdominal segments
cerci

chapter 1

MADE BY GOD

I was 26 years old and a mother of three children before I placed my faith in Jesus. By that time I had created and recreated an identity for myself many times over! In the late '60s I was obsessed with hippies. My family lived in Los Angeles and my step-father worked downtown. We often met him in Hollywood after work on Friday nights to see a movie. My mom would drive us in early to miss traffic and take us through the streets and shops. As we stood in line for movie premieres, my brother and I would watch the parade of fascinating people go by. The sidewalks were filled with hippies, and I would study them carefully. I loved their clothes, sunglasses, hats and attitudes, and I did the best I could to recreate myself into a mini hippy. In the '70s I wanted to be one of Charlie's Angels, specifically Farrah Fawcett. Though my hair was dark and thin and my teeth were crooked, I would study her image on the poster in my room and wish I could be just like her. The closest I got was learning to skateboard. In the early '80s I was captivated by the lead character in the movie Flashdance. You remember her—leotard, leg warmers and cut-up sweatshirt falling off one shoulder. There was always the desire to recreate myself, to start fresh, a new me with a new identity and the way people saw me and thought about me.

By the time God got ahold of me in 1989, I had no time for the luxury of defining myself. Now I was being defined by necessity. I was a wife and mom with three little kids and feeling very much like what is described in Genesis 1:2, "The earth was without form and void, and darkness was over the face of the deep." I was shell shocked by the reality of caring for kids, husband, pets and home. I was without form, feeling the void, and darkness covered the deep places in me. I cried out to Him, and in His mercy, He breathed life into me, filled me with His Spirit, marked me as belonging to Him and began to fill me with the knowledge of Him. He began to shape and mold me into the image of His Son. This also began the exciting discovery of who I am in Christ. The truth I discovered then, and hold dear today, is the fact that I am a new creation in Christ—old things are passing away, and I am experiencing all things becoming new. There have been many changes in me since that day. God had His work cut out with this restoration project! Looking back over the past 29 years I realize that many of the victories I have experienced in my personal growth and transformation have been a result of believing who God says I am in Christ.

WHO IS SHAPING YOUR IDENTITY?

Are you self-made? Our pride wants to take control and be the creator of our own image and the decision maker of purpose. Self wants to exalt itself and choose how it will express and present an image to others.

Self takes control to inform the world of identity through behavior, career, clothing, speech, material goods and social media outlets. When we doubt God is our creator, or fear what others think about us, we will shape an identity with our own hands. Pride will often drive a person to try to identify by saying, "What I do is who I am," but God's Word informs us that you can't do anything to become what you already are in Christ.

Are you man-made? People (parents, teachers, coaches, siblings, friends, co-workers, etc.) can leave their impression on us, informing and shaping our ideas of identity. Our world presents images, labels and language trying to push its mark upon us. Those in the world who reject God are lost, confused and empty and will grasp at the temporal to shape identity using things like money, fame, career, clothing, toys and branding.

Satan has had his thieving hands upon the identity of man since his first conversation with Eve. He has used lies to distort our perception of self, God and others. He is at work disconnecting mankind (the creation) from God (the Creator) thereby destroying the honor given to man having been made in God's image and subsequently the purpose of mankind. His lies are like a carnival mirror. We look at ourselves in that mirror and what we see is warped, not at all what our image truly is. Like everything else that is good, Satan steals, kills and destroys the honor and sanctity given by God of mankind's image.

Do you believe you are God-made? It was His hands that shaped and molded us. He has redeemed us from the curse and the sin that damaged our original identity. He is at work restoring our identity and purpose. His Word reveals the truth of our identity and His Spirit is at work transforming us so that we are a new creation in Christ being continually made new. He is renewing a right perception of Himself, others, self and nature.

1. In what ways have you tried to shape an identity for yourself?

2. What have been the results?

3. How have you seen the world exert its influence upon man's perception of self, God and others?

4. In what ways have you felt the influence of the world exert itself in shaping your identity?

5. What lies might you be believing about your true identity in Christ?

6. Why do you think Satan works at distorting our perception of our true identity in Christ?

MADE IN HIS IMAGE

In the beginning... there was no such thing as identity crisis! Preoccupation with self did not exist. There were no demands for "me time." Man and woman were simply a reflection of God, made in the image of their Creator. They were naked and not even aware of their nakedness—that is freedom!

They enjoyed fellowship with one another and communion with God. They understood their God-given occupation and were not rushed or stressed to do the work God had given them to do.

God reveals His presence and power through what He has created. When He formed man He did something unlike anything else, He made man in the image of Himself. We were made in His likeness, the very reflection of God, becoming the visible representation of the invisible God. Other creatures, the sky, the stars, the planets, trees and oceans all declare the glory of God, but only man is given the honor of being made in the image of his Maker.

And God saw everything that He had made, and, behold, it was very good.
Genesis 1:31a KJV

Read Genesis Chapters 1 and 2.

7. Record what you learn from Genesis 1:26–27.

8. What further insight are you given from Genesis 2:7 about God's creation of mankind?

9. Using what you have learned from Genesis 1:26, 27 and 2:7 describe in your own words God's creative process in making mankind.

10. How does acknowledging that you have been God-made, in His image, help to keep you from creating an identity for yourself?

11. What work did God give mankind to do? (Genesis 1:26, 28; 2:15–19)

12. God does not need help with stewardship. What does this say about God's desired original purpose for mankind?

Read Genesis 2:18, 21–25.

13. Describe how Adam and Eve related to one another.

14. Note what distinctions are given to mankind that sets him apart from the rest of God's creation.

15. How do those distinctions give value to your identity?

16. What have you discovered about your identity?

Knowing God's original design and intention for humankind is essential in understanding who we are in Christ. God doesn't make junk. He didn't start with a rough draft when He created Adam and Eve. He created them in His image. Understanding that man was made in the likeness of God brings value and honor to all people, not because all people behave in a way that is honorable, but because they were created by God as a reflection of Him.

All of creation reflects its Creator, but man bears the image of God—a special honor. Whether rich or poor, famous or unknown, young or old, male or female, every person has value because they bear the image of their Creator. Society labels people as "trash," "loser," "insignificant" or "unwanted," but if we acknowledge the label God attaches to every baby ever created, "MADE IN THE IMAGE OF GOD," we would recognize a precious piece of handiwork created by the Master. If we could see that label attached to humankind we would reverence every baby conceived as a precious, one-of-a-kind, treasure to be valued. We wouldn't destroy, discard, devalue, degrade, dishonor or disrespect an embryo, a child, a teen, a woman, a man, the elderly, the poor, the weak, the lame, the diseased.

Sin has marred the image of God in man and distorted the way we see Him, the way we perceive one another, the way we view nature and the way we see ourselves. We have been plagued by misconceptions of God since the serpent hissed the words, "did God really...?" We have blamed each other ever since for our own wrongdoing. We have tried to cover our flaws, our shame, and we have ruthlessly and selfishly exploited the very things we were given the privilege of managing. All the while our true identity has crumbled right under us.

> *Behold...*
> *But God showed his great love for us*
> *by sending Christ to die for us*
> *while we were still sinners.*
> *Romans 5:8 NLT*

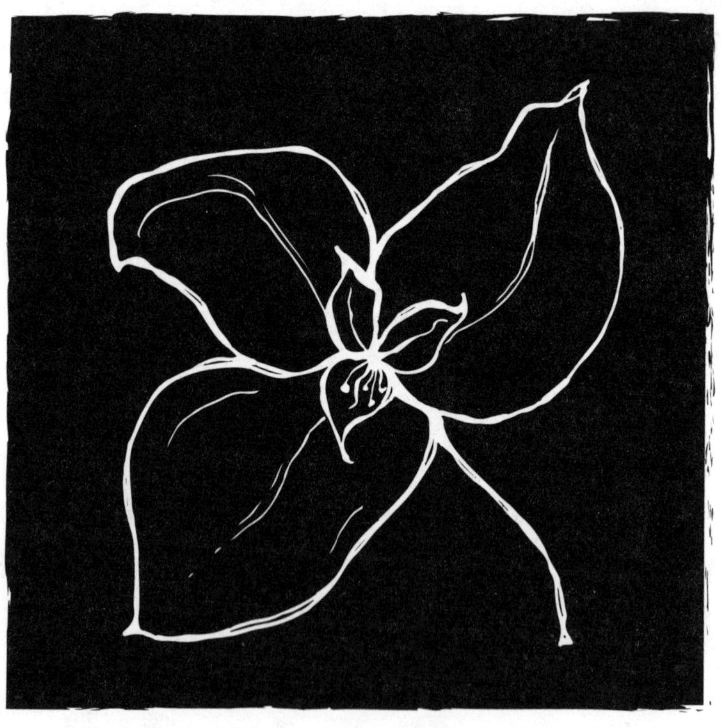

chapter 2

JESUS IDENTIFIED

...in these last days he has spoken to us by his Son, whom he appointed the heir of all things, through whom also he created the world. He is the radiance of the glory of God and the exact imprint of his nature, and he upholds the universe by the word of his power. After making purification for sins, he sat down at the right hand of the Majesty on high.
Hebrews 1:2-3 ESV

It was and is the ancient plan of God to redeem, restore and renew all He created. When Eve and Adam sinned, all of creation felt the effects. The fruit of the tree of the knowledge of good and evil was eaten, and the fade of the glory of creation began. Things began to crack and tear, room was made for distortion and corruption, and the slow process of death was in motion. But before that fatal bite was taken the Lamb of God was slain (Revelation 13:8).

When Eve and her man ate of the forbidden fruit, it killed their spiritual life. They were thrust out of their once glorious garden, banished from God's presence and mercifully denied access to the tree of life. Suddenly, tragically everything began to change. Have you ever done something so damaging in a relationship that it was ruined beyond your attempts to repair? This is what happened to Adam and Eve. There was no way for them to fix what they had broken. The way they saw and related to one another was damaged, the way they perceived God and their communion with Him was broken, even their relationship with nature was ruined.

Every generation since has inherited the sin-filled, corrupted nature of Adam and all the brokenness that comes with it. All men born of a woman have carried that flawed genetic code but One.

In the beginning was the Word, and the Word was with God, and the Word was God. He was in the beginning with God. All things were made through Him, and without Him nothing was made that was made. In Him was life, and the life was the light of men. And the light shines in the darkness, and the darkness did not comprehend it. John 1:1–5

And the Word became flesh and dwelt among us.
John 1:14 ESV

At a time determined by God, Jesus was sent to earth as the Redeemer. In His life as a man, Jesus would first identify Himself with mankind in order for mankind to be identified with Him. Through His death, the price of redemption would be paid so we could be reconciled to God. Through His resurrection, we have spiritual and eternal life, a new identity, a new relationship with God and the beginning of the restoration of all that was broken.

All our hope of life, healing, recovery, transformation, peace, significance, acceptance, and freedom is realized in Jesus Christ.

JESUS IDENTIFIED

1. Read the following verses and record what you discover about how Jesus identified Himself with humanity.
   a. Matthew 27:46, 50

   b. 2 Corinthians 5:21

   c. Galatians 3:13

   d. Galatians 4:4–5

e. Hebrews 2:18

f. Hebrews 4:15

Jesus identified with everything that marks our fallen identity. He was born a naked and helpless baby from a young, unwed Jewish woman. He identified Himself with the Jews, an Israelite, embracing Israel's national identity (known for their idolatry, lack of consecration, insignificance, weakness and slavery at that time in history). Jesus, clothed with humility and humanity, completely identified with man. No matter how weak, insignificant or low you feel, Jesus willingly chose to go lower. Jesus veiled himself in flesh. He is like us in every way. He knows what it is like to live, to lose, to die. He experienced rejection from His friends, peers, religious and political leaders, community and family. He felt the despise of those He loved. He was slandered, misunderstood and falsely accused. He knew what it felt like to be on the outside.

2. Record what you learn about Jesus from the following verses:
   a. John 12:45

   b. Colossians 1:15

    c. Hebrews 1:3

God made man in His image, and Jesus is the perfect man—the perfect image of God. Hebrews 1:3 says, Jesus is "the radiance of the glory of God and the exact imprint of His nature." This is Jesus: God incarnate.

God is restoring His image in us through the work of Christ by the power of the Holy Spirit.

3. Read the following verses and record what you discover.
    a. Romans 8:29–30

    b. 2 Corinthians 3:18

We can see all three persons of the Trinity involved in the restoration process. And it is the mighty power of His Spirit doing all the work. The Spirit is restoring everything that was broken: our perception of God and a loving relationship with Him, a right view of people and how we relate to them. Even our relationship to nature is being restored from selfish exploitation to a renewed appreciation and faithful stewardship. The conforming to Christ's image is something we experience here and now. Our original identity and original purpose have been recovered, and ultimately will be made better than the original. The completion of the restoration will take place when Christ returns.

4. Record the exciting truths you find in 1 Corinthians 15.
   a. Verses 21 and 22

   b. Verse 47

   c. Verse 48

   d. Verse 49

   e. Verse 50

   f. Verse 51

   g. Verse 52

> *And looking upon Jesus as he walked, he said,*
> *'Behold the Lamb of God.'*
> *John 1:36*

Believe it!
Was something uncovered about your identity in this chapter that is challenging your faith?

Enjoy it!
What did you behold about your identity in this chapter that has you excited?

Honor it!
Make a decision to honor God by choosing to believe what He says about who you are in Christ. Write your declaration: (i.e., I choose to honor Your Word, God, by believing You have made me a new creation in Christ.)

Observe it!
Hear and attend to what you learned from this chapter. Take a closer look, thoroughly examine what the Bible uncovers about God's ability, plans and purpose, Jesus' nature, or your identity. Do a word study, a character study. Is there more to uncover? Get curious!

Live it!
Choose to conform to your new identity by living it out.

Depend on it!
Is there anything that was uncovered in this chapter that seems impossible and yet is promised? Write out the promise and memorize it.

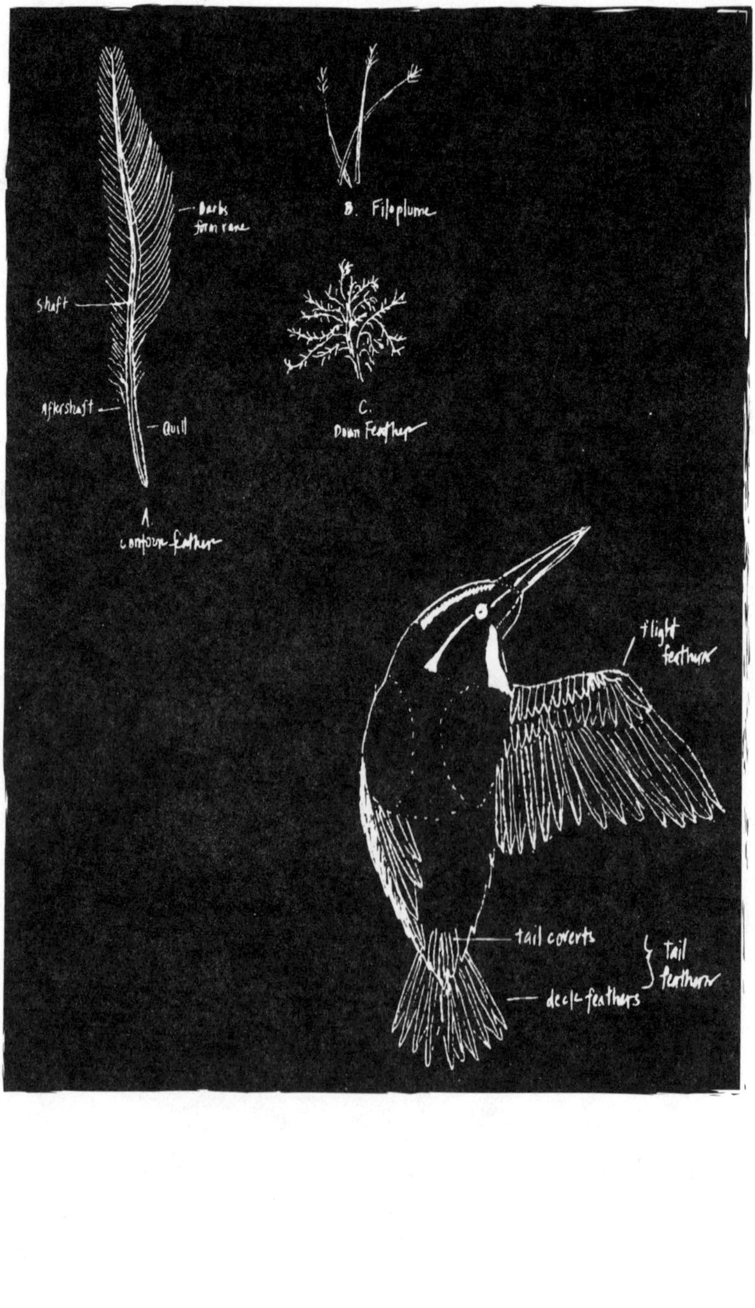

barbs
form vane
B. Filoplume
Shaft
Aftershaft
Quill
A.
contour feather
C.
Down Feather
flight
feathers
tail coverts
deck feathers
tail
feathers

chapter 3

I AM IN CHRIST

We know also that the Son of God has come and has given us understanding, so that we may know him who is true. And we are in him who is true by being in his Son Jesus Christ. He is the true God and eternal life.
1 John 5:20 NIV

When we place our faith in Jesus Christ, we are marked by His Spirit identifying us as belonging to God, accepted, secured and significant in Christ. All that we once were, or thought we were, begins to fade away and is replaced with a right perception of who God is and who we are in His Son.

Our identity remains elusive, like a dark shadow, until we are given the light of the Holy Spirit who reveals and illuminates Scripture so that we may see Jesus and behold who we are in Him. The Holy Spirit is needed to understand and believe, to reveal and convince that Jesus is who He says He is and we are who He says we are.

The one who is filled with God's grace and looks deeply into the face of Jesus in the Scriptures and is quickened by the Spirit to believe their identity in Christ will be made sure, steady and strong in their faith. Then, there is nothing that can talk that person down, no force on earth or sent from hell that can tell them differently. Once reshaped by the Master and fired in the furnace of faith you become solid. You can be called names, misunderstood, rejected by people, overlooked, left out, even verbally assaulted, but your roots go deep in Jesus. The core of your soul has the substance of faith and that integrity keeps you standing in the truth of who you are in Christ. Your feelings may be hurt but your faith in who you are will remain strong and steadfast.

> *Many times I have had to run back to God's Word and cry out to the Spirit, "Tell me again who You say I am and make me believe it!"*

It is God who has placed us in Christ and given the precious gift of His Holy Spirit to continually confirm and convince us of the truth of our identity in Him. It is the Spirit that imparts the spiritual vitality of Jesus in us so that we have a living union with Him. We are made partakers of His divine nature, not having some small part of Jesus, but having all of Jesus in us! It is in Christ that we are complete, holy and honored as a child of God. It's where we belong, are hidden and kept secure, given purpose and realize our significance. All of our identity is found in Him.

1. Read the following verses and record what you discover about a believer's union to Christ.
    a. Galatians 2:20

    b. Romans 6:4-5

    c. Ephesians 2:4-6

    d. Colossians 3:1

    e. Romans 8:17

Have you ever wondered if the Holy Spirit is living in you? How can you be certain?

God's Word tells us that we have been sealed with the Holy Spirit as God's way of giving us a pledge in the form of an earnest, like a down payment, of what God has promised will belong to us in heaven.

In Him you also trusted, after you heard the word of truth, the gospel of your salvation; in whom also, having believed, you were sealed with the Holy Spirit of promise, Who is the guarantee of our inheritance until the redemption of the purchased possession, to the praise of His glory.
Ephesians 1:13–14

In the ancient world, a seal was used to identify and to protect. If something was sealed, everyone knew who it belonged to (the seal had an insignia), and the seal prevented anyone else from tampering with the item. The Holy Spirit is upon us to identify us and to protect us.
David Guzik commentary, blueletterbible.org

To help identify the marks of that seal in your life consider the following questions and record your response.

2. Do you experience spiritual comfort that results in an encouragement and strengthening of your faith?

a. Read and record what you learn from John 14:16, 26; 16:7; 2 Corinthians 1:21, 22.

3. Since you placed your faith in Jesus have you experienced, and are you continuing to experience, a transformation of your heart and mind being conformed into the image of Jesus?

   a. Read and record what you learn from 2 Corinthians 3:18; 5:17; Philippians 2:13.

4. Do you understand the Word of God? Do you receive revelation and wisdom through the Bible?

   a. Read and record what you learn from John 16:13–16.

Through the Holy Spirit, we are experiencing a part of what we will experience in whole when we are in heaven. Now we have the Comforter and receive encouragement for our faith, in heaven we will experience everlasting joy. Now we are being transformed into the image of Christ by the Spirit; in heaven, we will experience perfect holiness. Now we have the light, guidance and tutoring of the Spirit to help us understand God. In heaven, we will live in the everlasting light of His presence.

The seal of the Holy Spirit proves that we are the real deal—the redeemed of God—we are not pretending to be holy and righteous. We are authentically and genuinely sanctified children of God, heirs and co-heirs with Christ. This is who we are and the Holy Spirit living in us is the proof that we belong to God, we are a part of His family, new creatures and His workmanship.

The Spirit is at work helping us to behold and believe these marvelous truths about who we are in Christ. We are about to tread on sacred ground, and we must be willing to let the Spirit of God remove our shoes, let go of our preconceived ideas, shed the layers of years and memories that would shroud the truth of our identity in Jesus. We will be required to walk by faith and not by sight, trusting in the power of God to renew the way we see Him, others and ourselves.

Being in Him changes everything about you! In Him, you become everything He created you to be.

> He is everything, and as we are joined to Him the
> poverty of our personal identity is lost in the fullness
> of His eternal greatness.
> Bob Sorge, Secrets of the Secret Place.

Are you unsure if God has given His Holy Spirit to live inside of you? Ask Him to settle this matter now. You can simply talk to Him and express your faith in His Son Jesus. Tell Him you joyfully receive the presence of His Spirit. Ask Him to open your spiritual eyes to see Him alive in you and He will do it!

Heavenly Father,

You are the Creator of all things and the Giver of life. Thank You for giving me spiritual life and placing me in Jesus—making us one. Please reveal the reality of Your Spirit living in me. Take hold of my heart and mind, and shape a right perception of who I am in You. Release me from bondage to the self-life and set me free to love You and others with abandon. In Jesus name, Amen.

> *And I will pray the Father, and He will give you another Helper, that He may abide with you forever— the Spirit of truth, whom the world cannot receive, because it neither sees Him nor knows Him; but you know Him, for He dwells with you and will be in you.*
> John 14:16-17

Believe it!
Was something uncovered about your identity in this chapter that is challenging your faith?

Enjoy it!
What did you behold about your identity in this chapter that has you excited?

Honor it!
Make a decision to honor God by choosing to believe what He says about who you are in Christ. Write your declaration: (i.e., I choose to honor Your Word, God, by believing You have made me a new creation in Christ.)

Observe it!
Hear and attend to what you learned from this chapter. Take a closer look, thoroughly examine what the Bible uncovers about God's ability, plans and purpose, Jesus' nature, or your identity. Do a word study, a character study. Is there more to uncover? Get curious!

Live it!
Choose to conform to your new identity by living it out.

Depend on it!
Is there anything that was uncovered in this chapter that seems impossible and yet is promised? Write out the promise and memorize it.

monarch caterpillar

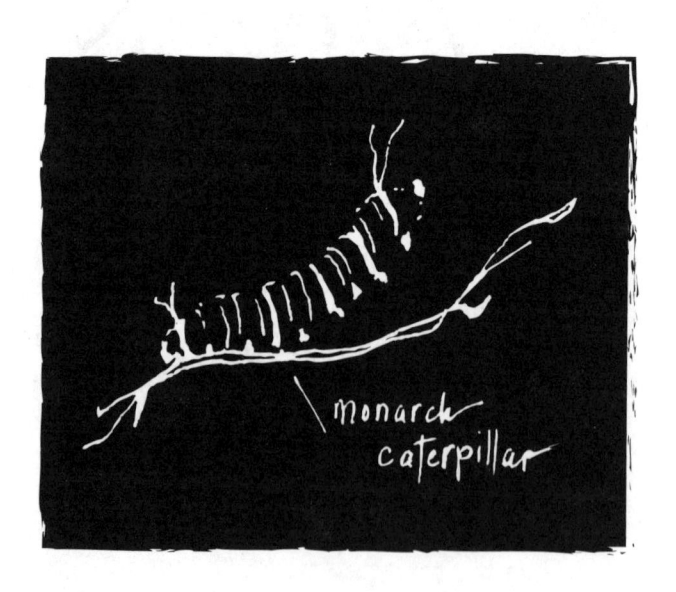

chapter 4

I AM ACCEPTED

To the praise and glory of His grace, wherein He has made us accepted in the Beloved.
Ephesians 1:6

If you have placed your faith in Jesus Christ you have been accepted by God and given forever, unconditional access to Him. The door to His throne room, His arms, His hands and heart are eternally open to you. He is ready to receive you. In fact, you have been received. The merits of Jesus have been ascribed to you making you acceptable to God. You have received God's grace, His Spirit, His gifts, sonship, purpose and an inheritance. When God took you as His own you were given His name and the reputation of Jesus.

In Christ is a constant reality for those who have placed their faith in Jesus. When we are saved we are forever embraced and firmly secured, after that separation from Christ becomes impossible. You are accepted continually and unconditionally. There is no force in heaven, on earth, nor power of darkness that is able to tear apart what God has joined together.

This truth of acceptance is the most vital of all aspects of our identity in Christ and upon which all other facets of our identity are secured. Our acceptance and access to God, by the grace of God through faith in Jesus, is a truth that is fiercely and relentlessly attacked, twisted, lied about and maligned by Satan.

Every man is given a seed of faith by God's grace and a free will to choose what to do with that seed. Will we put that seed in our pocket and forget about it, try to ignore it, or will we give it back to God?

There is nothing we are or can do that will open the door to gain access to God. Our acceptance and access to Him are granted to us when we place our faith in Jesus Christ's accomplishments upon the cross. Jesus finished all the work and left nothing to be done by us to gain God's favor. The gates were opened wide for all to enter, to come just as we are—weary, empty and at our worst. It is just the opposite of how we try to gain acceptance from others.

ACCEPTED BY GRACE

Read Ephesians 2:4-9

1. Why does God save?

2. Where does God place those He saves?

3. In Whom does God place those He saves?

4. What does God have planned in the ages to come? (verse 7)

5. How are we saved by God? (verse 8)

6. What has no part in God's salvation? (verse 9)

All God is looking for is that little seed of faith He gave to you. All of heaven waits to see with mounting anticipation, will you take that seed out of your torn and ragged pocket and give it back to God? When you do, heaven breaks out with shouts of joy and celebrating because you and God have been united!

*Those the Father has given me will come to me,
and I will never reject them.
John 6:37 NLT*

And now, encompassed by His grace, you are granted endless, boundless access to God, into His throne room, into His presence, onto His lap, into His heart and always on His mind. You are kept in His hand, as the apple of His eye, beyond your faithfulness to Him, extending beyond your good works, beyond your weaknesses, doubts, mistakes and failures.

You come by faith into His grace and by His grace you remain. You didn't slip through the cracks, you don't need to fear that you will be found out by Him, or that you have gone too far or that it is too late to come back to Him. Even when your heart, your mind and your obedience are far from Him He still has a hold of you. He is still always thinking of you. He never takes His eyes off of you. He doesn't play games, He doesn't punish, He doesn't ignore or get His feelings hurt. No,

He waits patiently, longing to be gracious, delighting to lower the ropes of His mercy, wrapped in His kindness, lifting you up in love and setting your feet on the solid ground of His truth. You are accepted by Him in Christ, and though people may reject you, some may turn their backs on you, you may be forgotten, overlooked, not noticed by those you love—with God, you are always welcome, always sought after, always brought near, always longed for with affection.

MADE BY GRACE

Whereby He has made us accepted.... Ephesians 1:6

> *Has made us accepted* is a Greek phrase meaning: to make graceful, lovely, charming, agreeable, acceptable. To pursue with grace, surround with favor, and honor with blessing.
> Thayer's Greek Lexicon

7. Read Ephesians 1:6. Write out the verse personalizing it.

8. By what means does God make us acceptable to Him? (Romans 5:1–2)

His grace has beautified you, making you lovely and agreeable in His sight.

Perhaps you have been plagued with thoughts of not being good enough, not lovable, not worthy of attention. We feel our inadequacy, we are in touch with our weaknesses and are aware of our shortcomings. We see them, Satan spotlights them, and people exploit them. God is the only one who can transform them, healing what is broken, filling what is lacking, strengthening what is weak, redeeming what is unworthy and beautifying it all!

You are graceful, lovely and charming to God. Everything about you has been made pleasing to Him. This is who you are in Christ. You may not feel it, but to build an identity upon how we feel about ourselves leaves us standing on ground that easily crumbles. We must pray for faith to believe we are who God says we are.

9. Why is knowing and believing that you are made accepted by God through His grace important to understanding your identity?

CHASED BY GRACE

We have all experienced it, the relentless pursuit of God's love and grace in our lives. And the pursuit didn't end when we surrendered our lives to Him. God's grace continues to persistently track our footsteps down every hill, up every mountain and through every valley. His grace has kept pace with our thoughts, ideas, imaginations and every attempt to form an identity apart from His truth.

10. Read the following verses and record what you learn about the pursuing grace of God.

   a. Psalm 23:6

   b. Ezekiel 34:11, 12

   c. Luke 15:4–6

   d. Romans 5:15–20

11. Why is the knowledge of God's grace continually pursuing you relevant to your identity in Christ?

Our identity is found in Christ. We will never know who we truly are apart from being in Him. God's grace is constantly at work chasing away thoughts of being separate and independent of Jesus. It is the voice of the enemy that tortures us with thoughts that we have gone too long or too far without church, worship, service, devotion or prayer. Satan's aim is to keep us away, creating an illusion of distance, a wide chasm between us and God which cannot be spanned because of sin and time. In Christ is a constant reality, transcending time and space. Separate from God is a lie. You may feel far away from Him, your affections may be consumed with someone or something else, your feet may have walked a great distance away, but you are firmly and forever planted in Jesus and accepted by God because of His abundant, ever-flowing, pursuing grace.

Indeed, we have all received grace after grace from His fullness.
John 1:16 HCSB

EMBRACED BY GRACE
Our very identity in Christ is encompassed by God's grace.

12. Read the following verses and record what you learn about the encompassing grace of God for those in Christ.

   a. Psalm 5:12

   b. Psalm 32:10

   c. Psalm 103:4

13. Why is knowing that you are continually surrounded by God's grace important to believing you have been made acceptable to God?

14. How might doubting this truth affect your relationship with God?

15. How might it affect the way you view yourself?

16. How do these truths affect the way you view others who have been made accepted by God?

God has united you with Jesus. You cannot be more accepted or given more access than you already have! Every bit of your being belongs to God and has been placed securely in Christ. He has become your dwelling place, a house for your soul and He has made you His dwelling place, a temple for Him to reside. He paid a great price to make you His home and the price for our place in Him was purchased by the same blood.

A person who has fully trusted in the merits of Christ, securely resting in His accomplishments on the cross, will be set free from self-effort, self-promoting, self-confidence, self-protecting and self-focus, free to be focused on Christ and others. The more we believe and trust in our acceptance and access to God by grace the less we will struggle with insecurity and fear. Boldness and confidence will bloom as we live in dependence upon Jesus and the beautiful fruit of peace and joy will be abundant.

> *For He says: "In an acceptable time I have heard you,*
> *And in the day of salvation I have helped you."*
> *Behold, now is the accepted time;*
> *behold, now is the day of salvation.*
> *2 Corinthians 6:2*

Believe it!
Was something uncovered about your identity in this chapter that is challenging your faith?

Enjoy it!
What did you behold about your identity in this chapter that has you excited?

Honor it!
Make a decision to honor God by choosing to believe what He says about who you are in Christ. Write your declaration: (i.e., I choose to honor Your Word, God, by believing You have made me a new creation in Christ.)

Observe it!
Hear and attend to what you learned from this chapter. Take a closer look, thoroughly examine what the Bible uncovers about God's ability, plans and purpose, Jesus' nature, or your identity. Do a word study, a character study. Is there more to uncover? Get curious!

Live it!
Choose to conform to your new identity by living it out.

Depend on it!
Is there anything that was uncovered in this chapter that seems impossible and yet is promised? Write out the promise and memorize it.

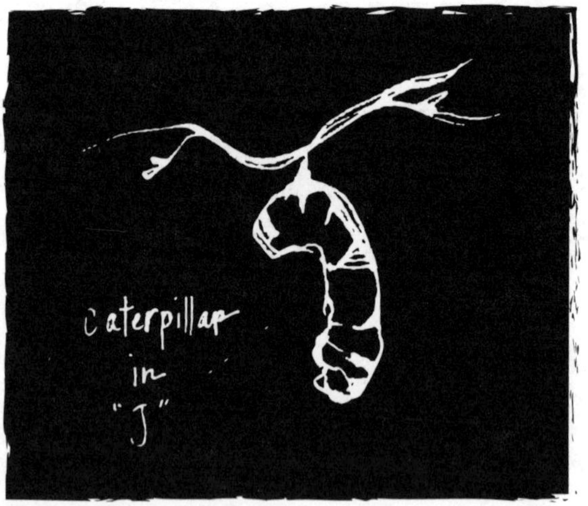
caterpillar
in
"J"

chapter 5

I AM JUSTIFIED

Being justified freely by His grace through the redemption that is in Christ Jesus.
Romans 3:24

The Holy Spirit is at work in our lives revealing the truths of our identity in Christ. God wants us to be assured of our acceptance and oneness in Jesus. He is giving us His eyes to behold ourselves the way He does. He sees us in His Son and never apart from Him. He wants to lift our focus up and out of self, onto Jesus. Our good Father knows how to free us from the fear of man and from the futility of the self-life.

1. What is justification?

2. How are we justified by God?

    a. Romans 3:22–28

    b. Romans 5:1–9, 18

    c. Galatians 2:16

3. What do you personally experience in your heart as a result of believing that your sins are forgiven and you have been declared eternally "not guilty" by God?

4. Read Romans 8:1. What has God removed from those who are in Christ Jesus?

5. What is condemnation?

6. As you meditate upon the fact that God has brought you into everlasting union with Him, what is produced in your heart and mind?

7. How might doubting that you are justified by faith in Jesus Christ affect your relationship with God?

8. How might uncertainty about your right standing with God affect your relationship with people?

9. In what ways does believing you have been justified by God give you confidence in your relationship with Him? In what ways does this free you from the need of "self-confidence" in drawing near to God?

God is never looking for worthiness in us but is continually looking upon the worthiness of His Son in us. If we are hesitating in approaching God because of feelings of unworthiness we have only to look again with eyes of faith upon Jesus—and keep them there!

Circle the statements you sometimes believe or do. Look up the verses attached to the statements you circled. Choose a verse to write out and memorize.

My sin or failure is more than God can forgive.
(Psalm 130:3–4; Romans 3:22–23)

I just can't forgive myself for what I have done.
(Romans 3:24–26)

I still feel guilty of my past sin.
(Isaiah 43:25; Hebrews 9:14)

I do not feel good enough for God to love me.
(Romans 5:5, 10)

I go to church and try to do as many good things as I can; I read my Bible and pray so that I can be right with God.
(Acts 13:39; Romans 3:28; Galatians 2:16)

---

*...Behold the Lamb of God, who takes away
the sin of the world.
John 1:29b*

Believe it!
Was something uncovered about your identity in this chapter that is challenging your faith?

Enjoy it!
What did you behold about your identity in this chapter that has you excited?

Honor it!
Make a decision to honor God by choosing to believe what He says about who you are in Christ. Write your declaration: (i.e., I choose to honor Your Word, God, by believing You have made me a new creation in Christ.)

Observe it!
Hear and attend to what you learned from this chapter. Take a closer look, thoroughly examine what the Bible uncovers about God's ability, plans and purpose, Jesus' nature, or your identity. Do a word study, a character study. Is there more to uncover? Get curious!

Live it!
Choose to conform to your new identity by living it out.

Depend on it!
Is there anything that was uncovered in this chapter that seems impossible and yet is promised? Write out the promise and memorize it.

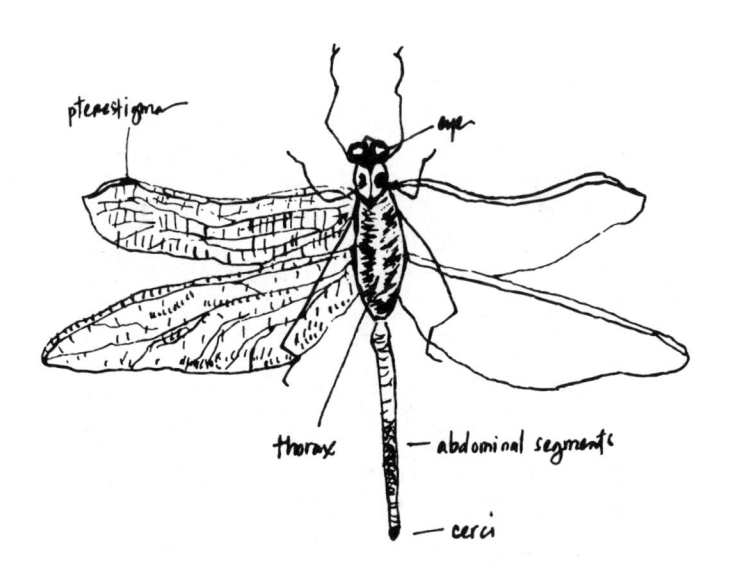

chrysalis

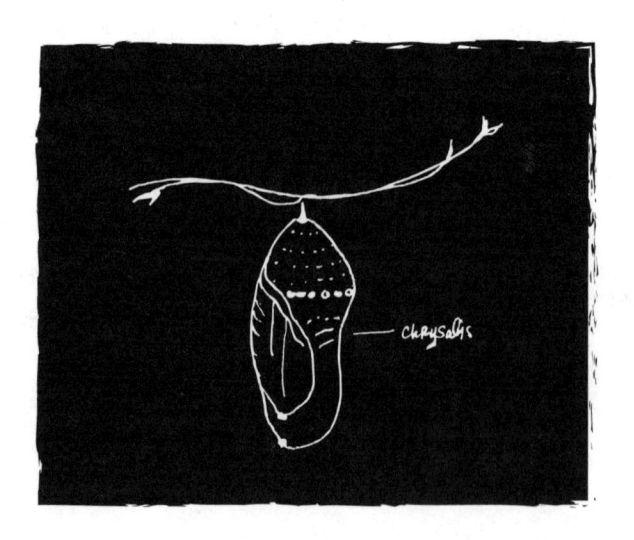

chapter 6

I AM GOD'S CHILD

Behold what manner of love the Father has bestowed on us, that we should be called the children of God.
1 John 3:1

A need to be accepted and a desire to belong are hardwired into every soul. God made us this way! We were designed to belong to our Heavenly Father, to enjoy an intimate loving relationship with Him and with others.

The honor of being a son or daughter of God is something we must behold and take hold of! Once this single truth is locked down by faith it will be all the esteem, worth and confidence we will ever need.

As daughters and sons of God, we have been given life-changing favor and eternal benefits. Our Father wants us to not only know who we are but what we have as His child.

We have been given the honor of being called His child. He gives this title to those He esteems above others and shows it by His love, favor, protection and benefits.

1. How does one become a child of God?

    a. Galatians 3:26

    b. John 1:12–13

2. Use the following verses to describe God as a Father.

    a. Psalm 68:5

b. Luke 11:9–13

   c. Luke 15:11–24

   d. James 1:17

3. What benefits and favor have you been given as God's child?

   a. John 1:16

   b. Ephesians 1:3–14

   c. 1 Peter 1:3–5

d. Revelation 21:6

4. What other benefits or privileges do you possess as His child?

5. How do you know you are His child?

   a. Romans 8:14–17

   b. Galatians 4:6

6. Respond to 1 John 3:1–2

Our Father sent His Son to die for our sins and proved on the cross just how much we are worth to Him. He paid the redemptive price for our lives and it was no less than Jesus' life and blood. There is nothing more valuable and it is proof of our worth to God.

As children of God, we get to be just that—a child! Before we became God's children we were fending for ourselves in life. What a sacred crisis we come to when we come to an end of ourselves and the beginning of a life of faith and dependence upon our Father in Heaven!

7. How does your confidence in this unbreakable, grace-filled, Father–child relationship affect the way you relate to God?

8. How does it affect the way you relate to people?

Circle the statements you sometimes believe or do. Look up the verses attached to the statements you circled. Choose a verse to write out and memorize.

My Heavenly Father expects me to take care of myself.
(Psalm 55:22; Isaiah 46:4; John 10:11)

God favors some of His children over others.
(Deuteronomy 10:17; Romans 2:11; 1 Peter 1:17)

God does not care about me.
(1 Peter 5:7)

I don't feel favored by God.
(Psalm 5:12)

I struggle to come to God with my problems.
(Matthew 7:7; 11:28; 21:22)

I am sometimes punished by God.
(Psalm 119:71; Proverbs 3:12; Hebrews 12:5, 11)

I don't feel like I am cherished by God.
(Psalm 42:8; 103:2, 4; Jeremiah 31:3)

I don't feel like I am a part of God's family.
(Galatians 3:26; Ephesians 2:19; 1 John 3:1)

I question whether God really has a place for me in Heaven.
(Philippians 3:20; John 14:1–3)

I doubt that God has an inheritance for me in Heaven.
(Ephesians 1:11; 3:6)

I struggle to relate to God as a Father and me as His child.
(Galatians 4:6; 1 John 5:1)

9. How does knowing and believing that you have been accepted by God and made His child satisfy your desire to belong? Does it satisfy you?

Spiritual adoption takes place at the time of salvation. The one placed by God into His family immediately receives all the privileges and freedom of being His child.

We do not merit or earn our way into God's family but are purposefully and permanently placed by His power and authority. As His child:

> He claims us as His own (1 Peter 2:9–10).
>
> He brings us near (Ephesians 2:13).
>
> He takes responsibility for our well-being (Psalm 23).
>
> He cancels the debt we owed for our sins (Colossians 2:14).
>
> He loads us up with benefits (Psalm 68:19; Ephesians 1:3, 11).
>
> Not only clears our record of wrong but gives us Jesus' record of right (1 Corinthians 1:30).
>
> He makes us spiritually alive (Ephesians 2:5).

His grace superabounds and is super-amazing! It not only pays our debt, but takes our zero balance and adds, heaping up good things, benefits, honor, and an eternal inheritance for each one of His children.

From the beginning Satan has appealed to our prideful nature, speaking lies to promote independence from our Heavenly Father. Ideas like self-esteem, self-worth and self-confidence have slithered into our churches, homes and minds and have no biblical foundation. Our source of confidence, worth and esteem are found in Christ alone! We have only to BEHOLD what manner of love the Father has given to us.

> *Behold what manner of love the Father has bestowed on us,*
> *that we should be called the children of God.*
> 1 John 3:1

Believe it!
Was something uncovered about your identity in this chapter that is challenging your faith?

Enjoy it!
What did you behold about your identity in this chapter that has you excited?

Honor it!
Make a decision to honor God by choosing to believe what He says about who you are in Christ. Write your declaration: (i.e., I choose to honor Your Word, God, by believing You have made me a new creation in Christ.)

Observe it!
Hear and attend to what you learned from this chapter. Take a closer look, thoroughly examine what the Bible uncovers about God's ability, plans and purpose, Jesus' nature, or your identity. Do a word study, a character study. Is there more to uncover? Get curious!

Live it!
Choose to conform to your new identity by living it out.

Depend on it!
Is there anything that was uncovered in this chapter that seems impossible and yet is promised? Write out the promise and memorize it.

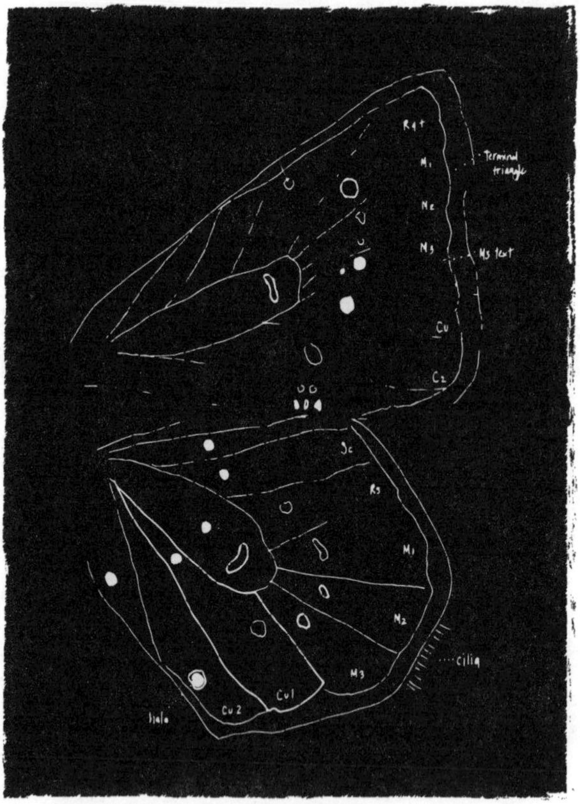
R4+
M1
Terminal triangle
M2
M3
Cu
C2
Sc
Rs
M1
M2
M3
cilia
Cu1
Cu2
halo

chapter 7

I AM A NEW CREATURE

Therefore, if anyone is in Christ, he is a new creation; old things have passed away; behold, all things have become new.
2 Corinthians 5:17

Our nature is what makes us "us." It includes all the character qualities that make us who we are. And while we truly are uniquely made, one thing we all have in common is that we are born sinful. The Bible tells us that every human being is born with Adam's nature, a sinful nature bent toward rebellion and self-pleasing. When God saves us we receive a new nature and His Spirit begins a radical spiritual transformation work in us.

One of the most exciting and promising facts of our identity is that we are a new creation in Christ! This one truth is full of dynamite power, in fact, just the kind of power it would take to make those who are spiritually dead alive in Christ. It is the mighty power of God that makes us an entirely new creature, transforming us into the image of Jesus. Nothing less than the almighty power of God can heal, erase and remove the effects of sin and corruption, carrying us past these things and move us forward as a new creation to a new life in Christ. In Christ, we will experience old things pass away and behold all things becoming new.

1. Record what you learn from the following verses about God's power at work in a believer.

    a. Romans 8:9–11, 29

    b. 2 Corinthians 3:18

    c. Ephesians 1:19–20

We are not imitators of Christ, trying to be like Him, God is making us like Him. The same power that raised Jesus Christ from the dead is living in us, transforming us into the image of Christ.

2. What were some of the first things you beheld of the Holy Spirit transforming you into a new creation?

3. How were you able to determine that this was a work of God's power and not a work of your flesh?

4. According to the following verses what has God made new in you?

   a. Ezekiel 36:26–27

   b. Romans 12:2

   c. 2 Corinthians 5:17

d. Ephesians 4:24

e. Colossians 3:10

f. 2 Peter 1:4

OLD THINGS HAVE PASSED AWAY

In 2 Corinthians 5:17 we are told: "old things have passed away." Old things refer to time, conditions and the things of men. It includes our old sin nature and the effects that sin has had upon us. God's power is able to reach beyond time, to trace and touch points of origin in our life so that there is not an old place, time or condition in us that He is not able to make pass away. The idea behind this phrase pass away means that His power has the ability to not only omit the damaging effects from your old life but to carry you past them and continue to move you forward.

Do you need the almighty power of God to reach and touch old things in you? If so, write out a prayer asking Him to do that work in you. He is more than able to heal and carry you beyond the pain and devastation of your past and He longs to lift you up and move you forward. His power is also able to break old sinful habits and tendencies.

5. Read Colossians 3:1–14.
    a. What things are we told to put to death and put off? (Verses 5, 8 and 9)

    b. What reasons are given for not behaving in these ways?

    c. What are we told to put on?

The phrase *put on the new* (verse 10) was used in Paul's day to refer to putting on a new set of clothes. There are some old behaviors of our old nature that do not suit us as any longer, they should feel uncomfortable because they don't match up with our new identity.

6. Read verse 10 and explain what this means in your own words.

We are new creatures in Christ with a free will to choose what behaviors we will take off and what we will put on. When we choose to identify with Jesus we are given the grace and power to put off and put on.

7. Read and record the facts, promises and encouragement from these verses:

   a. Romans 12:1–2

   b. 1 Corinthians 1:30

   c. Philippians 1:6

   d. Philippians 2:13

   e. 2 Peter 1:3–4

8. Do your habits, patterns and behavior reflect that they are identified with Jesus? What old clothes are hanging around that need the help of God's power to be taken off and made to pass away? These are clothes you

don't want to give away or store away, they need to pass away!

How we respond to our flaws and weaknesses is important. We can't excuse them as just being human, and beating ourselves up over them does no good either. Our flaws must be recognized for what they are: unsurrendered parts that need to get into the Master's hands. They need the power and grace of our Creator to be made new. We may feel the pressure of His Spirit and Word at work in our life, but we can trust His process. He who began that good work of grace in us will be faithful to complete it!

In Chris Tiegreen's devotional book *Heaven on Earth*, he says, "That frustrating finiteness, those limitations we accepted as "normal," those flaws we embraced as "only human"—all are temporary exceptions to our created design. We were made for so much more." He goes on to say, "Most practices and disciplines do more to highlight our futility than they do to empower us for glory. The only way we experience either freedom or glory is by being so thoroughly filled with and saturated with the Spirit of the King that we step into an entirely new state of being. It's a new dimension of living. And it's no longer frustrating and futile."

ALL THINGS HAVE BECOME NEW AND ARE BECOMING NEW

9. Read 2 Corinthians 5:17.

    a. What things are becoming new?

b. What would that include?

c. Are there any things God cannot or will not make new?

The form of the verb *are become* communicates a continual becoming new.

10. What new work is God doing in you presently?

11. What new work would you like God to do in you?

12. Is there anything you are struggling to believe God will change in you?

13. Gather and record wisdom and encouragement from Isaiah 43:18–19.

> *I see my faults: I talk too much, I lack grace, I express and exert my opinions, I give unsolicited advice (this is just the short list!). I want to change, I tell myself I will change! Only to fail again. O God, take this lump of clay—remember I am but dust—warm me in Your hands, pour Your water over me, reshape me into the image of Your Son and fire me in Your furnace.*

Circle the statements you sometimes believe or do. Look up the verses attached to the statements you circled. Choose a verse to write out and memorize.

There are some things in me that will never change.
(Ephesians 3:20; Philippians 1:6)

There are some things in other people that God cannot change.
(Jeremiah 32:17; Luke 1:37; 18:27)

It is up to me to change myself.
(Ezekiel 36:26; Romans 12:2; Ephesians 4:23; Titus 3:5)

There are wounds so deep in me that God cannot reach to heal.
(Psalm 103:3; Malachi 4:2; Luke 4:18)

When we feel our insufficiency, insecurity or the hostile takeover of the old man/woman, we can go back to God's Word, listen to His voice, search for His opinions, seek for His truth and ask God to help us believe He is working in us to renew, restore, recreate, revive and restore us into the image of Jesus. Instead of beating ourselves up, trying to punch a new nature out of the old clay we can ask God to reshape and make new. We will never get a new response out of an old nature. If we recognize that there is something in us that does not look, sound or feel like Jesus, that is a place to ask The Potter to take ahold of and make new by His grace and power.

> *Where there is true faith, there is new birth, and that term implies a change beyond measure complete and radical.*
> *Spurgeon*

Nothing is impossible for God! Not only does He have life-giving and life-changing power, He loves to make something from nothing! He can bring things from death to life. There is hope for relationships to be renewed, lives to be changed, hearts to be healed. There is nothing too small (not even DNA), or too big, or too difficult that He cannot rewire, reorder or recreate! He delights in opening new doors, bringing us in to new seasons, using us to blaze new trails. He is passionate about creating and building, and He desires to use us in His life-changing work. Has God been inspiring you to do something new?

*Then He who sat on the throne said,
"Behold, I make all things new."
And He said to me,
"Write, for these words are true and faithful."
Revelation 21:5*

Believe it!
Was something uncovered about your identity in this chapter that is challenging your faith?

Enjoy it!
What did you behold about your identity in this chapter that has you excited?

Honor it!
Make a decision to honor God by choosing to believe what He says about who you are in Christ. Write your declaration: (i.e., I choose to honor Your Word, God, by believing You have made me a new creation in Christ.)

Observe it!
Hear and attend to what you learned from this chapter. Take a closer look, thoroughly examine what the Bible uncovers about God's ability, plans and purpose, Jesus' nature, or your identity. Do a word study, a character study. Is there more to uncover? Get curious!

Live it!
Choose to conform to your new identity by living it out.

Depend on it!
Is there anything that was uncovered in this chapter that seems impossible and yet is promised? Write out the promise and memorize it.

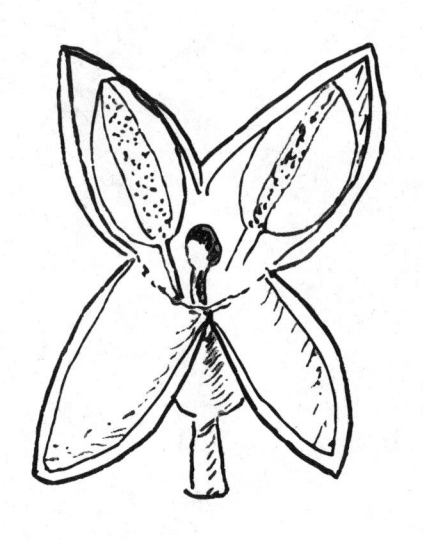

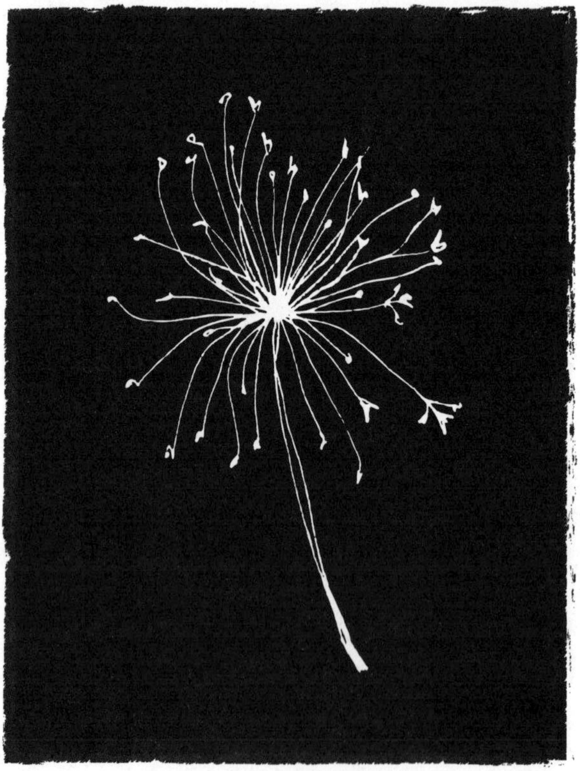

chapter 8

I AM COMPLETE

For in Him dwells all the fullness of the Godhead bodily; and you are complete in Him, who is the head of all principalities and power.
Colossians 2:9-10

When we begin to understand and believe that we are complete in Christ we will be set free from the fear of not being or having enough. We will be able to let go of lifelong habits and the bondage of trying to measure up and striving to be more.

Christ is enough, therefore we are enough and have enough. He has given everything: His life, His power and His nature. We have been given everything that pertains to life and godliness. We are perfect and perfected in Christ and though we eagerly await the completion of His completion in us—our faith and trust in the finished work is the solid ground we stand on in the meantime. By the grace of God, I am what I am: a work in progress but good as done.

We sometimes may feel a need to cover up or mask our weaknesses and flaws. We think we must appear to be a good Christian, something we feel we are not. We know we are a saint in Christ, but we don't feel saintly. Discovering our true identity in Christ, believing, not feeling we are who God says we are, gives us the freedom to take off the Christian costume and rest in the reality of being complete in Him.

Read Colossians 2:9–10

The word *complete* means "to cause to abound, richly furnish, to render perfect, fulfill, to fill to the top so that nothing shall be wanting."

1. Using this definition of *complete* write out Colossians 2:9–10 personalizing the verses.

2. Read Hebrews 10:10–14 and record what you learn about the sufficiency of Christ to perfect you.

3. Looking at the history of the church, what behaviors of man can you observe have been an attempt to add or subtract from the finished work of Jesus?

Attempts to attach a work of the flesh to the finished work of Christ on the cross will still leave a person wondering if that work is enough. Those who believe that Jesus was enough and did enough in His life, death and resurrection will live with the peace and rest that comes from knowing sufficiency in Him.

4. Read the following verses and record what you learn.

a. John 1:16

b. 2 Corinthians 12:9

c. Ephesians 1:3

d. Ephesians 1:17–23

e. Ephesians 3:14–21

f. Colossians 1:19

g. 2 Peter 1:3

Jesus is the only truly satisfying thing in life. Everything else eventually falls short. Christ is our only hope for fulfillment. There is nothing that is capable of filling and satiating the soul of man but the indwelling—filled to the fullness—of Christ in us. Some religions and religious activities may bring a degree of light to some parts but will leave other parts in the dark; they leave some things dependent upon man to fulfill. But for those in Christ, the all-sufficiency of God is able to fill all in all, able to fill the complexity and entirety of a man. The body, soul, and spirit of redeemed man are filled, made to abound and rendered perfect.

When a person is born into the family of Christ it is then that he is complete in Christ. His spiritual growth is not by addition, but nutrition. He grows from the inside out. Nothing needs to be added to Christ because He is already in the very fullness of God. And as the believer draws on Christ fullness, he is filled into all the fullness of God; what more does one need?
Warren Wiersbe.

5. What behaviors do you sometimes see in yourself that don't reflect a belief that Jesus is enough?

If you need encouragement to believe the outstanding truth of being complete in Christ take some time to meditate on some of the truths of the New Testament that use this same word *complete* (from Colossians 2:10) to tell of what we have in Christ. Acts 2:28; 13:52; Romans 15:13–14; Philippians 1:11; 4:19; 2 Thessalonians 1:11.

Circle the statements you sometimes believe or do. Look up the verses attached to the statements you circled. Choose a verse to write out and memorize.

I need to pay for my mistakes.
(Isaiah 53:5; Hebrews 10:10; 1 Peter 3:18)

I need to deny myself something to gain something from God.
(2 Corinthians 9:8; Ephesians 1:3)

I need more to feel good about myself.
(Colossians 2:9–10)

I need something I don't have in order to please God.
(Romans 15:13; Hebrews 11:6; 2 Peter 1:3)

I need more to do more for God.
(John 1:16; Romans 8:32; 2 Corinthians 12:9; Philippians 4:19)

I need to do more for God.
(John 6:29; Galatians 2:16; 2 Thessalonians 1:11)

We all have little parts inside that need to be convinced that we are who God says we are: Complete in Christ. They are places that need to be surrendered and committed into the Master Shaper's hands. Take this warped, misshapen piece in me Father and mold it into the image of Christ.

Arise, believer! And behold yourself 'perfect in Christ'
Let not your sins shake your faith
in the all-sufficiency of Jesus.
You are—with all your depravity—
still in Him and therefore complete.
You have need of nothing beyond what there is in Him.
In Him—at this moment—you are entirely clean...
In Him an object of divine approval and eternal love.
As you are...and where you are...you are still complete.
Feeble, forgetful, frail, fearful and fickle in yourself,
Yet in Him

> *You are all that can be desired*
> *Your unrighteousness is covered*
> *Your righteousness is accepted*
> *Your strength is perfected*
> *Your safety is secured*
> *Your heaven is certain.*
> *C. Spurgeon*

Behold...
His divine power has given to us all
things that pertain to life and godliness,
through the knowledge of Him who called
us by glory and virtue,
by which have been given to us
exceedingly great and precious promises,
that through these you may be partakers
of the divine nature,
having escaped the corruption that is in
the world through lust.
2 Peter 1:3-4

Believe it!
Was something uncovered about your identity in this chapter that is challenging your faith?

Enjoy it!
What did you behold about your identity in this chapter that has you excited?

Honor it!
Make a decision to honor God by choosing to believe what He says about who you are in Christ. Write your declaration: (i.e., I choose to honor Your Word, God, by believing You have made me a new creation in Christ.)

Observe it!
Hear and attend to what you learned from this chapter. Take a closer look, thoroughly examine what the Bible uncovers about God's ability, plans and purpose, Jesus' nature, or your identity. Do a word study, a character study. Is there more to uncover? Get curious!

Live it!
Choose to conform to your new identity by living it out.

Depend on it!
Is there anything that was uncovered in this chapter that seems impossible and yet is promised? Write out the promise and memorize it.

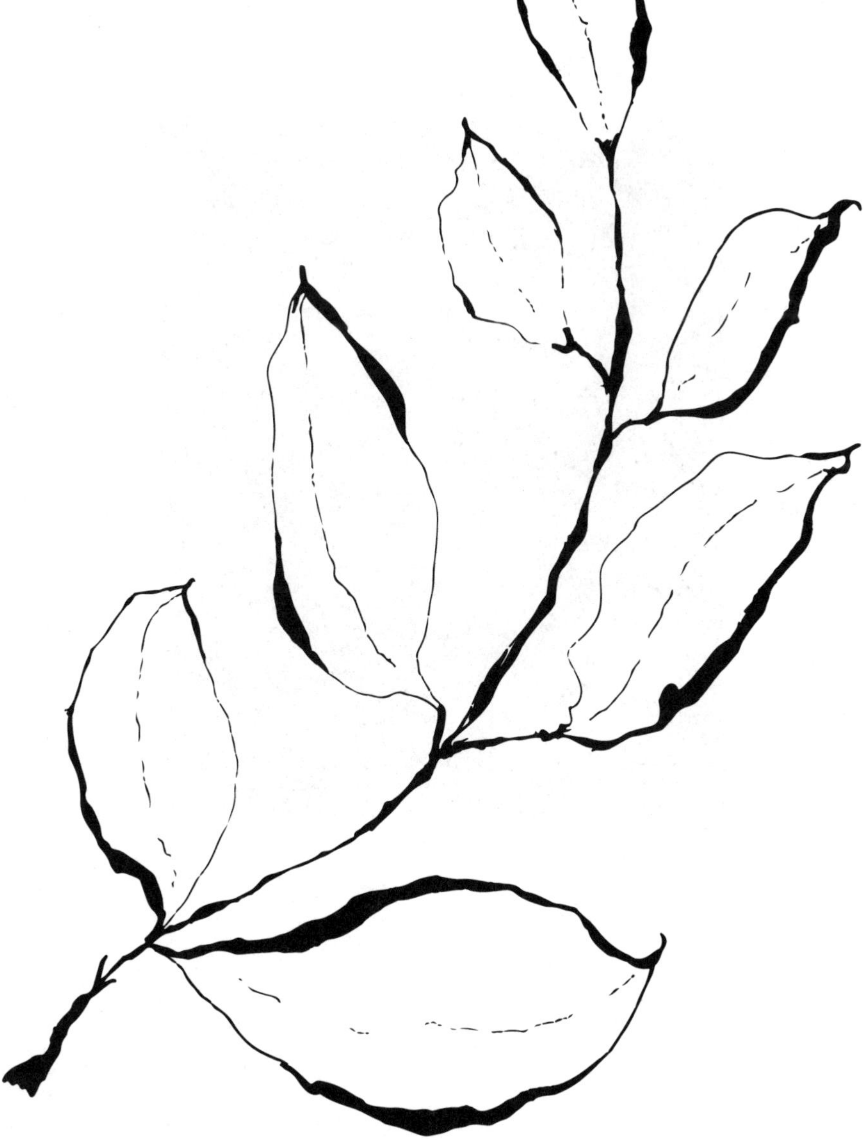

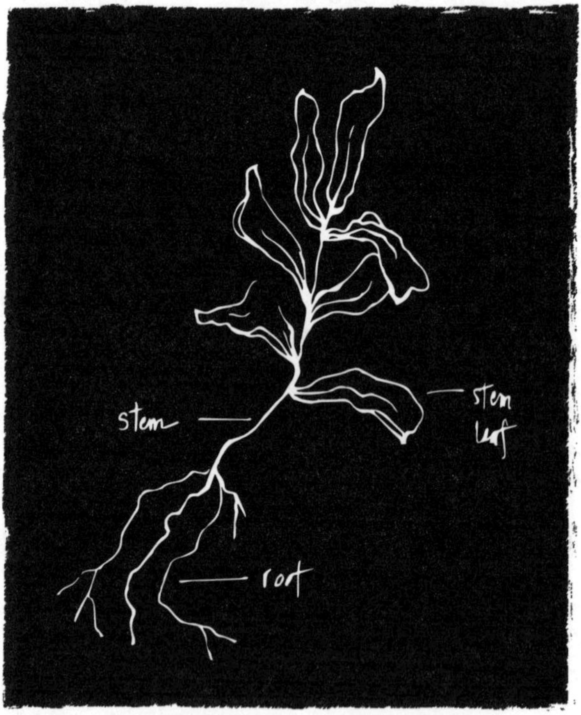
stem
stem
leaf
root

chapter 9

I AM SECURE

Blessed be the God and Father of our Lord Jesus Christ, who according to His abundant mercy has begotten us again to a living hope through the resurrection of Jesus Christ from the dead, to an inheritance incorruptible and undefiled and that does not fade away, reserved in heaven for you, who are kept by the power of God through faith for salvation ready to be revealed in the last time.
1 Peter 1:3-5

One of the most powerful and dramatic changes experienced by a Christian comes when finally convinced by the Holy Spirit of being eternally secured in Christ. As we begin to believe that we are always and forever in Him, super-glued, sealed and secured, positioned in Christ by faith we can rest from striving to earn and maintain a place in Him.

In Christ is a constant reality. It is a constant that cannot be broken or altered by time, behavior, external conditions, internal feelings or spiritual forces of darkness. God is strengthening our faith in the reality of His faithfulness and power to keep us in Christ. As we grow in our trust of this fact we are free to look away from self-confidence and place all our confidence in the power of God to keep us securely in Christ. We don't have to pep talk, rally or positive think our way into anything. We are free to rest in Jesus as we believe He was good enough and did enough to secure a place in Him.

When we look inward to find something of value in and of ourselves, something we feel we need to keep us in Christ, we will either fall into an abyss of emptiness, unable to find anything of worth, or we will splash into an abundance of natural born talent, aptitude, intelligence and full of self—we feel we are enough and have enough. In either case looking inward to find worth only keeps us in chains to the self-life, bound to independence, in an illusion of separateness from Jesus. It is vital to our spiritual well being that we behold ourselves always with and in Christ, always attached to Him and unable to do anything apart from Him.

Insecurity is born and bred in the darkness of fears that arise from the uncertainty of our security in Christ. Being separated from Christ would require someone or something that has the power to pry open the hand of God!

1. Our position in Christ is secure. Read the following verses and record what you learn about your union with Christ.

   a. 1 Corinthians 6:17

   b. Ephesians 2:6

   c. 1 Corinthians 1:30

2. Read the following verses and record your thoughts concerning the certainty and security of the bond we have with Jesus.

   a. John 10:28–29

   b. Romans 8:38–39

   c. Ephesians 1:13–14

Read Ephesians 1:3–6.

3. When did God plan and prepare a place for us in Jesus?

The foundation of the world is mentioned in Scripture as the extreme borderline of the past from which human history is reckoned. We were present in the mind of God and loved by Him before He founded the world! It was at that ancient time He determined that we would be placed in Christ.

4. Record your response to the facts of Ephesians 1:3–6.

5. What attitudes and behaviors might develop in a person if they are doubting the security of the bond they have with Jesus?

6. What truths about the security of your position and inheritance in Christ need to be strengthened in you?

God wants to settle this fact of our identity once and for all! When we truly begin to believe that Jesus did enough and is enough for all we will ever need and that we are forever one with Him we will be released to participate in the purpose for which He created us!

Certainly God is so chained, and so linked, and so nailed to His people by His everlasting love, and by His everlasting covenant, and by the blood of His Son, and by His oath, and by that law of relation that is between Him and them, that no created power shall ever be able to deprive them of Him.
Thomas Brooks

Behold...
And I give them eternal life, and they shall never perish; neither shall anyone snatch them out of My hand. My Father, who has given them to Me, is greater than all; and no one is able to snatch them out of My Father's hand. I and My Father are one.
John 10:28-29

Believe it!
Was something uncovered about your identity in this chapter that is challenging your faith?

Enjoy it!
What did you behold about your identity in this chapter that has you excited?

Honor it!
Make a decision to honor God by choosing to believe what He says about who you are in Christ. Write your declaration: (i.e., I choose to honor Your Word, God, by believing You have made me a new creation in Christ.)

Observe it!
Hear and attend to what you learned from this chapter. Take a closer look, thoroughly examine what the Bible uncovers about God's ability, plans and purpose, Jesus' nature, or your identity. Do a word study, a character study. Is there more to uncover? Get curious!

Live it!
Choose to conform to your new identity by living it out.

Depend on it!
Is there anything that was uncovered in this chapter that seems impossible and yet is promised? Write out the promise and memorize it.

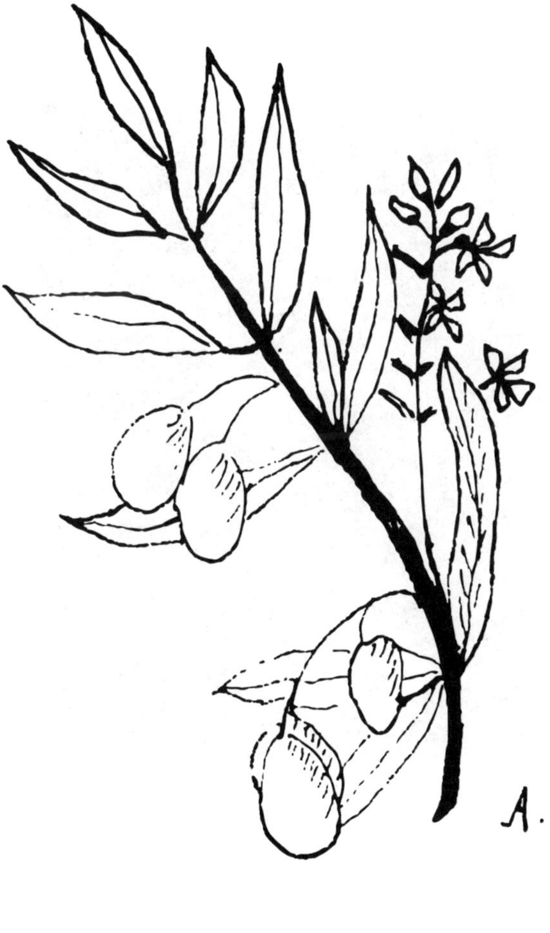

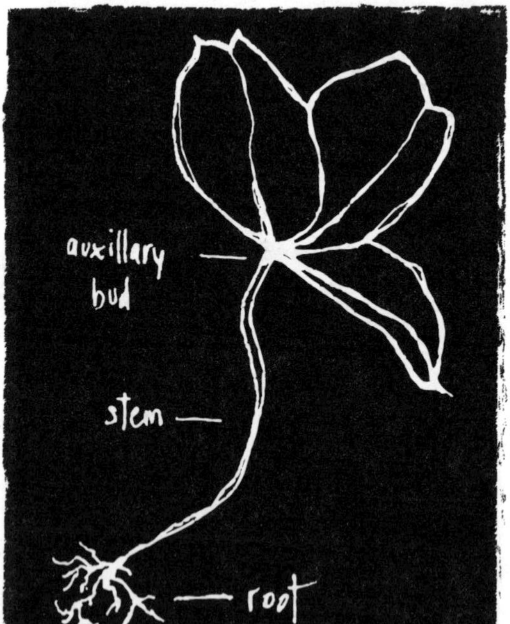
auxillary bud
stem
root

chapter 10

I AM ROOTED

...that He would grant you, according to the riches of His glory, to be strengthened with might through His Spirit in the inner man, that Christ may dwell in your hearts through faith; that you, being rooted and grounded in love, may be able to comprehend with all the saints what is the width and length and depth and height—to know the love of Christ which passes knowledge; that you may be filled with all the fullness of God.
Ephesians 3:16-19

Recently I attended a beautiful art show filled with young, interesting people. A man and woman were playing soft, calming music using small bowls, a tuning fork, a drum and a large gong. People from the crowd laid on the ground next to the musicians. I hadn't seen something like this since my mini hippie days. They were sound bathing, a practice that allows sound vibrations to wash over the body and soul, believed to bring balance, calm and creative inspiration. I live in California where everything old is new again (if you are my age). It is not surprising to see a generation that has been chronically exposed to technology, hyper-social activity, rapidly changing environments and the pace and push of living in our area, seeking to find some way of grounding.

Without Christ, we feel our vulnerability in an ever-changing world. We sense we are without roots and we try to fill our lives with things that we hope will have the weight and substance our souls need to feel calm and secure. Some roam the earth barefoot trying to collect an electric charge to ground themselves, others meditate, massage, mantra, sound bathe, vacation or retreat to rid themselves of the constant noise that can make a soul spin. We are inundated with opinions, changes and global shifts that try to pull us one way and then another. The very earth under our feet seems to crumble at times and we can feel like all is slipping into the sea.

We need our soul anchored to the Rock of Ages. Without Him we sway and drift, we feel as though we are floating, adrift upon the sea of life—we grab for devices to keep us on top of the water while inside we fear what we cannot see in the dark below. The flux of life can have a powerful influence over a life and identity that is not grounded in Jesus and His love.

God has permanently united His children to Jesus. Our lives are so completely intertwined and tangled together with Him that we have become one. We have been absorbed right into the fibers of Jesus, no longer two separate beings with two different identities, not just wrapped around Him, but swallowed up and into Him. Our souls are so completely infused with His that there is not a piece or place in us that is not filled with the life of Christ. In Jesus, we are kept from the push and pull of the world and Satan.

1. Read Ephesians 3:16–19.

   > Strengthen (Ephesians 3:16)
   > To strengthen, make strong, increase in vigor, to empower.

   a. What part of our being is built up by God?

   b. What is the inner man?

   c. Through what power are we strengthened?

   d. What is Paul's expressed desire for this prayer? (verses 17–19)

Paul is asking God to help us comprehend the love of Christ. He is asking that we not only know the love of Christ but that we would apprehend and take possession of His unconditional and immeasurable love.

> Rooted (Ephesians 3:17)
> Greek= Rhizoo
> To cause to strike root, to strengthen with roots, to render firm, to fix, establish, cause a person or thing to be firmly grounded.

2. Why is it important for you to know that being rooted in Jesus means you are rooted in love?

3. What effects might it have on a person if they doubt they are rooted in the love of Christ?

> Grounded (Ephesians 3:17) To lay the foundation, to make stable, establish.

4. We are also grounded in the love of Jesus. As you take possession of this fact, what does it produce in you?

5. In your own words describe what it means to be filled with all the fullness of God. (verse 19)

6. Fill in this equation:

   Jesus + _____=Fullness

7. What are you tapping into as a source of inner strength?

8. Where do you plant yourself to find peace?

9. To what do you attach yourself to acquire stability?

10. What makes you feel secure about your well being?

11. Are there parts of your life you might be "outsourcing" to find love, healing, peace, security, or strength?

In Christ we not only have a place to keep us safe and secure, steady and stable but we also have a place of resource. Once grafted into Him by the grace of God we are continually in the source and supply of life. The life of Jesus in us is so abundant and so alive that it is always growing, forever supplying so that His life is continually expanding in us and out of us!

12. What does God supply for those who are in Christ?

　　a. Ephesians 3:20

　　b. 1 Corinthians 1:3–9

　　c. Philippians 4:19

　　d. 2 Peter 1:3

13. What is God building up in us?
    1 Peter 2:4–5

14. In what ways can we cooperate with the Holy Spirit in the strengthening of our inner man?

    a. Matthew 7:24–25

    b. John 15:4–5

    c. Jude 20–21

15. Write out and personalize the promises of Jeremiah 17:7–8.

Rapid change, ever-increasing exposure to social shifts, instability of a worldwide political climate and the internal undercurrent that drives many to stay relevant—all of it can leave us feeling like we don't have ground under our feet. We need the grounding effect of being rooted in Jesus. His roots are all-powerful, never-changing eternal roots. He is the self-existing One, the One whose Being reaches backward forever, forward indefinitely, higher than can be known and lower than is fathomable. When we place our faith in Him our soul and spirit are hidden in Him. We no longer need to search for a source from the outside to bring calm, balance, strength, creativity and healing to our inside. We have the presence of the Holy Spirit living in us. He is the continual life-giving source of our spirit, body and soul.

You have a secure place in Jesus with roots to keep you steady, stable and strong. You are tapped into the greatest creative source that exists and grafted into the One who heals you from the inside out. Christ in you and you in Christ, together all the fullness of God dwells.

> Circle the statements you sometimes believe or do. Look up the verses attached to the statements you circled. Choose a verse to write out and memorize.
>
> I must take care of myself.
> (1 Peter 5:6–7)
>
> I must make sure that I save and reserve (money, resource, time, energy) for future needs.
> (Philippians 4:19)
>
> God helps those who help themselves.
> (Psalm 46:1, 10; Matthew 5:5)

God + _____ = Inner Strength
(2 Corinthians 12:9)

I can become more stable and grounded by incorporating something from the world into my life.
(Colossians 2:10)

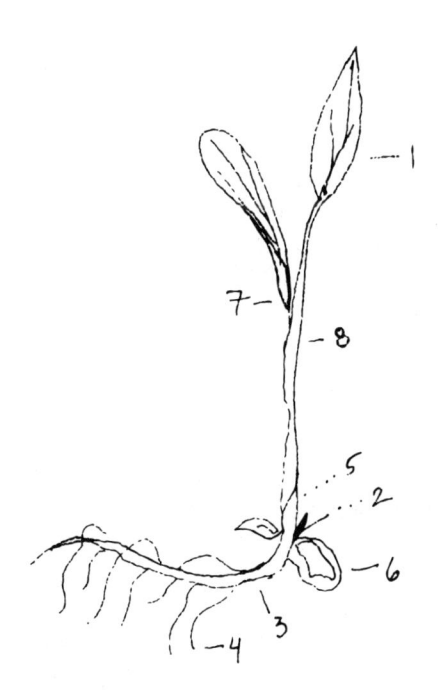

> *And behold, I am with you always,*
> *to the end of the age.*
> *Matthew 28:20b ESV*

Believe it!
Was something uncovered about your identity in this chapter that is challenging your faith?

Enjoy it!
What did you behold about your identity in this chapter that has you excited?

Honor it!
Make a decision to honor God by choosing to believe what He says about who you are in Christ. Write your declaration: (i.e., I choose to honor Your Word, God, by believing You have made me a new creation in Christ.)

Observe it!
Hear and attend to what you learned from this chapter. Take a closer look, thoroughly examine what the Bible uncovers about God's ability, plans and purpose, Jesus' nature, or your identity. Do a word study, a character study. Is there more to uncover? Get curious!

Live it!
Choose to conform to your new identity by living it out.

Depend on it!
Is there anything that was uncovered in this chapter that seems impossible and yet is promised? Write out the promise and memorize it.

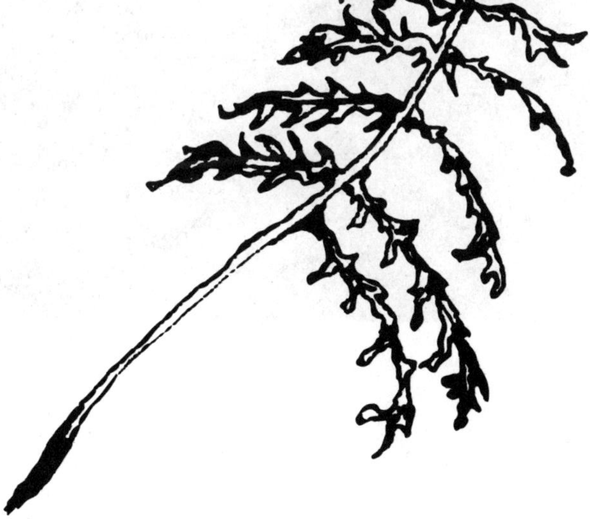

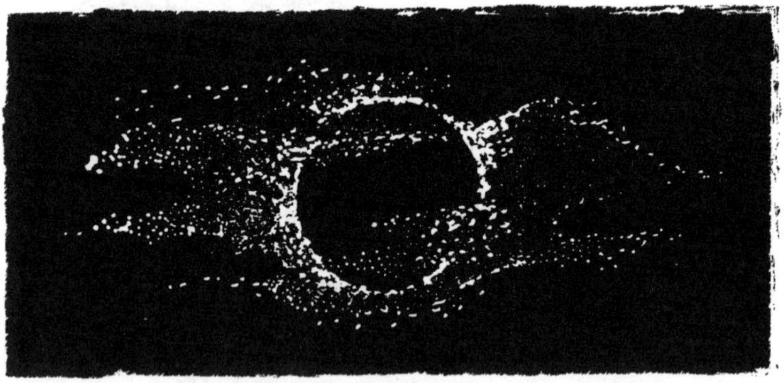

chapter 11

I AM MORE THAN A CONQUEROR

Yet in all these things we are more than conquerors through Him who loved us.
Romans 8:37

Though we don't always feel like a mighty conqueror, in fact, some days and even seasons we may feel more like a war-torn and wounded warrior, the truth is we are standing in victory when we are positioned in Christ.

It is impossible for anything or anyone to separate us from our place and identity in Him and because of that fact we live in and from a place of victory. We are identified as more than a conqueror through Christ because we are in Christ.

1. Read through the following verses in Romans chapter 8. Next to each verse, note what has been conquered for you through Christ.

    a. Verse 31

    b. Verse 32

    c. Verse 33

    d. Verse 34

    e. Verse 35

    f. Verse 37

g. Verse 38

2. What does 1 Corinthians 15:54-57 and Colossians 2:15 confirm about the victory of Jesus?

We are more than a conqueror through Christ because the victory of Jesus not only canceled out the debt we owed for our sin, not only defeated sin, death and Satan but also opened a way for His grace to be received.

> More than a conqueror is a Greek phrase meaning: overwhelming victory, to gain a surpassing victory, super victory.

3. In what ways are we made more than a conqueror through the grace of Jesus?

   a. 1 Corinthians 1:30

   b. Ephesians 1:3-14

   c. Philippians 3:20

     d. 1 Peter 2:10

Fear was a part of our old nature and identity. We once were held captive by Satan and made a slave to fear. We feared death, damnation and eternal separation from God. The victory of Jesus has set us free from that bondage and given us a new Spirit. Now our relationship to God has changed, once He was our Just Judge, now He is our Loving Father.

4. Read Romans 8:14–17 and record what you discover.

     a. How is your life reflecting the truths of these verses?

5. What do the following verses say we conquer, overcome and triumph in, through Christ?

     a. 1 John 4:2–4

     b. 1 John 5:4–5

c. Revelation 12:10–11

6. How do these verses encourage you?

The Holy Spirit has been given to us to be a continual witness of the victory of Jesus. He has been given to help us experience the reality of that victory while proceeding through life on earth.

> *But thanks be to God, who in Christ always leads us in triumphal procession, and through us spreads the fragrance of the knowledge of him everywhere.*
> *2 Corinthians 2:14 ESV*

> Leads us in triumphal procession is a Greek phrase meaning: causes us to triumph, causes us to celebrate a triumph, a victory hymn sung in procession.

7. Describe a time when you have experienced God causing you to celebrate and sing with Him as He led you through a difficulty.

We lose nothing that we have or are in Christ when we go through even the most difficult things in life. We not only lose nothing but we gain peace, joy and more faith. We are made more than conquerors in Christ Jesus.

As God leads us through the trials and tribulations of this life, opening our spiritual eyes to see the reality of the victory He has already secured for us, it will cause us to celebrate here and now. This is why we can count it all joy when experiencing trials of many kinds: they are opportunities to catch a glimpse of the Victor and the victory, and we will joyfully proceed singing the song of triumph with Him.

8. Why is it important for you to believe that being more than a conqueror is who you are in Christ?

Circle the statements you sometimes believe or do. Look up the verses attached to the statements you circled. Choose a verse to write out and memorize.

I feel like I'm losing the battle more than winning or conquering.
(1 Corinthians 15:57; 1 John 4:4)

I am being defeated in everything I set out to do.
(2 Corinthians 2:14; 1 John 5:4)

It feels like everything/everyone is against me.
(Romans 8:31; Hebrews 13:6; 1 John 4:4; 5:4–5)

I fear man.
(Psalm 118:6; Proverbs 29:25; Matthew 10:28; Romans 8:31)

I fear death.
(1 Corinthians 15:54; 2 Corinthians 5:8)

I fear pain.
(Isaiah 43:2)

I fear the future.
(Isaiah 41:10, 13; Matthew 10:31; Luke 12:7)

I fear the struggles/circumstances my family is going through will destroy us.
(Isaiah 44:8; Romans 8:35–37)

It is the Holy Spirit working within the believer obtaining the victory for the believer. No strategy is seen, no battlecry is heard and yet the victory is secured. Spurgeon

God has already positioned us on the Victor's side, He is just patiently waiting for our surrender and cooperation to proceed with Him. When we believe we are more than a conqueror in Christ Jesus, living in that fact, we will experience the Holy Spirit transforming us into the image of Jesus in an ever-increasing glory! Our true identity will emerge reflecting the identity of Jesus. We will join in the victory song—our heads will be lifted, not in pride, but in joyful, triumphant procession singing with Jesus all the way Home.

But one of the elders said to me, "Do not weep. Behold, the Lion of the tribe of Judah, the Root of David, has prevailed to open the scroll and to loose its seven seals."
Revelation 5:5

Believe it!
Was something uncovered about your identity in this chapter that is challenging your faith?

Enjoy it!
What did you behold about your identity in this chapter that has you excited?

Honor it!
Make a decision to honor God by choosing to believe what He says about who you are in Christ. Write your declaration: (i.e., I choose to honor Your Word, God, by believing You have made me a new creation in Christ.)

Observe it!
Hear and attend to what you learned from this chapter. Take a closer look, thoroughly examine what the Bible uncovers about God's ability, plans and purpose, Jesus' nature, or your identity. Do a word study, a character study. Is there more to uncover? Get curious!

Live it!
Choose to conform to your new identity by living it out.

Depend on it!
Is there anything that was uncovered in this chapter that seems impossible and yet is promised? Write out the promise and memorize it.

— chrysalis

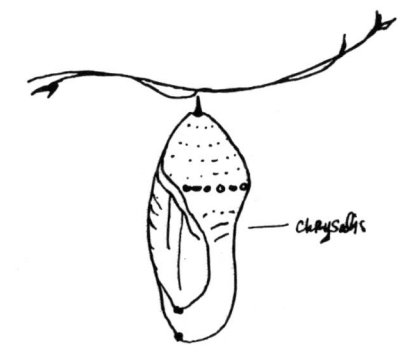

Corn

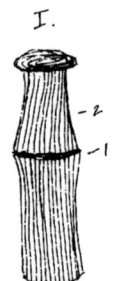

I. Stem
  1. node
  2. internode

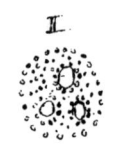

II. Transverse Section of Vascular Bundle

III. Longthwise Section of Vascular Bundles

IV. Seedling
  1. Plumule
  2. Caulicle
  3. Primary root
  4. Secondary roots
  5. Adventitious
  6. grain of Corn
  7. node
  8. internode

V. Sprout
  1. Caulicle
  2. Plumule
  3. endosperm
  4. root

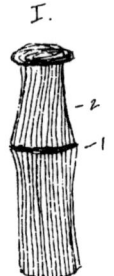

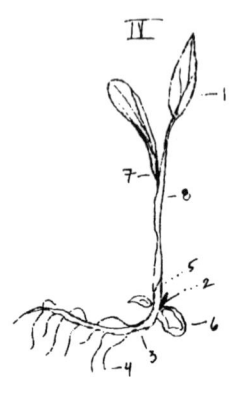

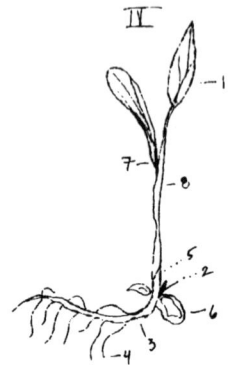

chapter 12

I AM SIGNIFICANT

But you are a chosen people, a royal priesthood, a holy nation, God's special possession, that you may declare the praises of him who called you out of darkness into his wonderful light.
1 Peter 2:9 NIV

God's Holy Spirit is at work in us revealing our identity in Christ and strengthening our faith to believe what He says is true about who we are in Him. He is establishing these truths deep within, providing us with what we need to make us stronger and steadier in our identity. God's grace eraser is removing misconceptions and lies that mar the image of Him and our identity in Him. He is replacing it with a right perception of who He is and who we are in Christ. And these truths are setting us free so that we can take hold of that for which Christ has taken hold of us.

In Christ, we become a significant part of God's purpose and plans. God has always wanted a people that represent the reality of His presence, power and love and a people that reflect His glory. He is getting us free from the self-life! Self-focus only breeds anxiety, minimizes fruit bearing and chokes out the life of Christ in us. A person who is at peace with their identity in Christ will possess a joyful confidence in their place in Christ. They will be able to rest and remain in Him, live a life that is flourishing, like a well-watered garden, free from the worry of being enough, having enough or doing enough—Christ has become everything.

One of the greatest victories we can experience as a Christian is to be free from the fear of man, and knowing who we are in Christ is key! Paul knew this to be true in his life. He purposefully detached himself from his pre-Christ identity. He saw the things that shaped his identity in the world as a hindrance to his spiritual growth and usefulness to God.

We rest and remain in Him by faith and He produces fruit in our lives that reflects the reality of His presence and power. We rest in Him and everywhere we go the fragrance of Christ fills the air. We rest and trust in Him and He exerts His influence on us to cooperate in His purpose.

1. Read the following verses and record what you discover about God's plans and purpose for your life.

   a. Matthew 5:13-14

   b. John 15:8

   c. 1 Corinthians 3:9

   d. 2 Corinthians 5:20

2. Read 1 Peter 2:9-10.

   a. How does Peter identify God's people?

A chosen generation refers to those who have obtained salvation. We have been given access to God, our King, to offer spiritual sacrifices and therefore called to be a part of

His royal priesthood. We are a holy nation because God has separated us from the world and set us apart for His plans and purpose. We are called a peculiar people, or God's own special possession because we have been redeemed and now belong to Him.

    b. How do these truths of your identity bring significance to who you are in Christ?

    c. What purpose is assigned to our identity? (verse 10)

3. Read Philippians 3:3–14.
    a. What did Paul declare in verse 12?

    b. What things did he feel necessary to leave behind? (verses 4–7)

    c. How might Paul's reaching behind to his identity in the world hinder him from moving forward in his calling and purpose in Christ?

4. Read and respond to 1 Corinthians 1:26–31.
   a. What kind of behaviors might develop in a person who doubts they have significance and purpose in Christ?

   b. In what ways does believing you have significance and purpose in Christ affect your:

   Behavior

   Priorities/Pursuits/Passions

   Dependency on God

It is not what we do as a Christian that determines who we are—it is who we are in Christ that determines what we do. God has placed us, by His grace, in Christ, given us a high, holy and heavenly calling, so we honor our position in Him. We don't serve God to gain acceptance, we are accepted therefore we serve. We don't follow Him in order to be loved, we are loved and therefore we follow Him.

monarch
caterpillar

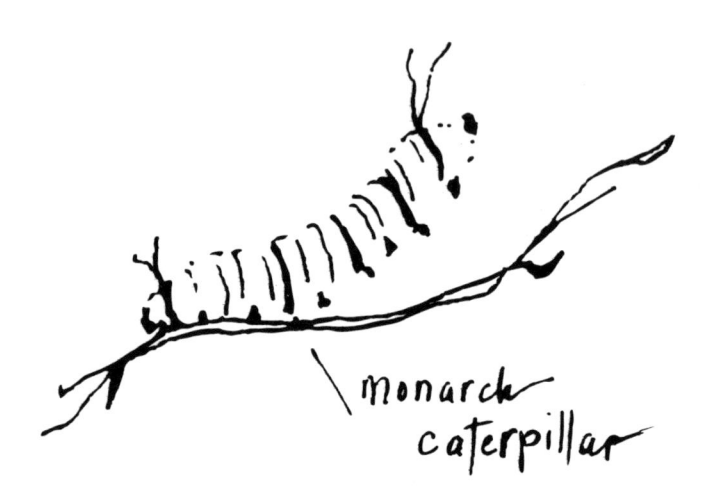

> *Behold...*
> *...you are a chosen people,*
> *a royal priesthood, a holy nation,*
> *God's special possession,*
> *that you may declare the praises of*
> *him who called you out of darkness*
> *into his wonderful light.*
> *1 Peter 2:9 NIV*

Believe it!
Was something uncovered about your identity in this chapter that is challenging your faith?

Enjoy it!
What did you behold about your identity in this chapter that has you excited?

Honor it!
Make a decision to honor God by choosing to believe what He says about who you are in Christ. Write your declaration: (i.e., I choose to honor Your Word, God, by believing You have made me a new creation in Christ.)

Observe it!
Hear and attend to what you learned from this chapter. Take a closer look, thoroughly examine what the Bible uncovers about God's ability, plans and purpose, Jesus' nature, or your identity. Do a word study, a character study. Is there more to uncover? Get curious!

Live it!
Choose to conform to your new identity by living it out.

Depend on it!
Is there anything that was uncovered in this chapter that seems impossible and yet is promised? Write out the promise and memorize it.

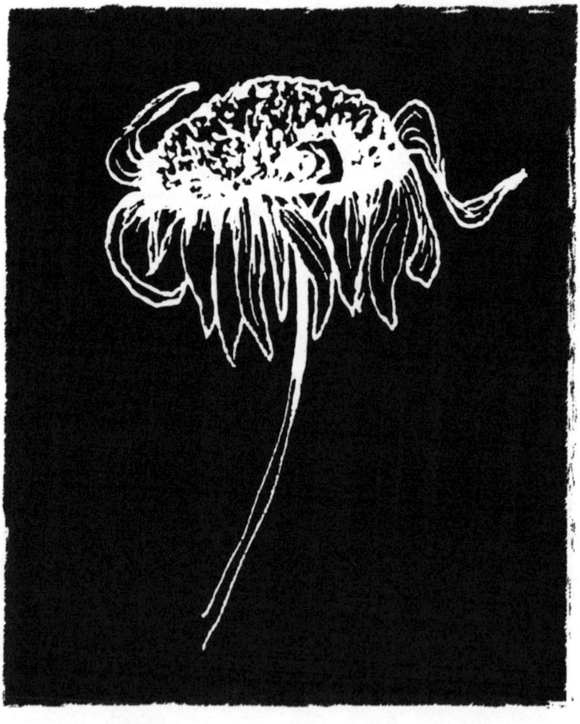

chapter 13

I AM A MASTERPIECE

For we are His workmanship, created in Christ Jesus for good works, which God prepared beforehand that we should walk in them. Ephesians 2:10

God stands alone as the Point of Origin of all things ever created. All hands, minds and inspiration find their beginnings in Him. He is the Master Craftsman and you are His greatest work.

You are a living, breathing, piece of art—God's masterpiece. Every detail of your being has been carefully considered; you are a fresh and original thought of the Originator of All. How many are Your thoughts, O God? He has authored an eternal poem's worth. He is like a Maestro, collecting and arranging music notes, stringing them together, making a melody of your life that is in harmony with Him. Both form and function were in His thoughts as His ancient hand designed you. You are not only beautiful to behold (and who would dare say that God does not make all things beautiful), you have been skillfully equipped for the Master's use.

The word *workmanship* comes from the Greek word *poema*, meaning "that which is made." This word is used only twice in the New Testament and connects creation with its Creator, capturing the Master in His artful creative energy and identifying Him as the mind and power behind the work.

If we trace our origin back to a black hole or a black blob, to places that are void and without form, we will see ourselves void and without form. It's no wonder that the enemy of God has been out to obscure, distort and created man's view of the hand of his Creator. Until we acknowledge the Author of all creation as our Creator we will slavishly work at filling that void, attempting to fashion an image for ourselves. We are witnessing this very thing in our world today as man tries to remove God, rejecting and denying Him as Creator, feverishly, pridefully, fearfully fumbling to assign an imagined identity to himself/herself/itself/other (you choose).

> *Workmanship* here in Ephesians 2:10 refers to the spiritual creation resulting from the regenerative work of God in human life.

Just as the words of Psalm 100:3 refer in similar terms to the first creation of humankind, so here Paul points to humanity's recreation in Christ as being wholly divine work. —W. G. M. Martin, "The Epistle To The Ephesians," in F. Davidson, ed. *The New BIBLE Commentary,* (Grand Rapids: Wm. B. Eerdmans, 1953), p. 1020.

1. Take a moment to prayerfully meditate on the truth of Ephesians 2:10, "For we are His workmanship."
    a. Describe what it means to you to be a divinely inspired work of God.

    b. Why is it crucial to your identity in Christ to acknowledge God as your Creator?

    c. Who or what have you allowed to shape an image for you?

An author is one who has authority over his work and decides how it will be used.

    2. Does your life reflect that God is the Author of it?

    3. Who is the one in authority over the decisions of how you spend your time, energy and gifts?

    4. Why is it important to acknowledge that God is the Author of your life?

    5. Where is the workmanship created?

        a. Why is this significant?

We understand from Ephesians 2:10 that our lives are fashioned by God, belonging to Him and made with a purpose.

6. What is that purpose?

7. When were these good works prepared for you?

8. Read Psalm 139:16.
   What is stirring inside you as you consider that God has prepared and pre-ordained work specifically planned for you to do?

9. Read Ephesians 2:4–7 and 3:7–11 and see if you can discover some of the grand and marvelous plans and purposes of God for making us His workmanship in Christ.

Circle the statements you sometimes believe or do. Look up the verses attached to the statements you circled. Choose a verse to write out and memorize.

I determine what I will do with my time, energy and gifts.
(Romans 11:36; 1 Corinthians 6:19; 2 Corinthians 5:15; Colossians 1:16)

There is nothing unique or special about me.
(Psalm 139:13–17; 1 Peter 2:9)

I have difficulty believing anything good can come from my life.
(John 15:16; 1 Corinthians 1:7-9, 27-28; 2:9)

I feel like my life has no purpose or significance.
(John 15:5, 8; 2 Corinthians 5:18; Philippians 2:13; 1 Peter 2:9)

If all of creation reveals the handiwork of God, how much more the redeemed soul of man. We have been created in the very image of our Creator, made with the capacity to know, understand and relate to the One who made us. Redeemed man is truly a wondrous work to behold! Humanity was made to display God's glory and grace.

In all of creation, there is not a flower, mountain, ocean, natural phenomenon or expansive galaxy that could ever compare to the workmanship of a soul that has been redeemed and transformed by the love and power of God.

I AM A MASTERPIECE

> Behold...
> You made all the delicate, inner parts of my body
> and knit me together in my mother's womb.
> Thank you for making me so wonderfully complex!
> Your workmanship is marvelous—how well I know it.
> You watched me as I was being formed in utter seclusion,
> as I was woven together in the dark of the womb.
> You saw me before I was born.
> Every day of my life was recorded in your book.
> Every moment was laid out
> before a single day had passed.
> Psalm 139:13-16 NLT

Believe it!
Was something uncovered about your identity in this chapter that is challenging your faith?

Enjoy it!
What did you behold about your identity in this chapter that has you excited?

Honor it!
Make a decision to honor God by choosing to believe what He says about who you are in Christ. Write your declaration: (i.e., I choose to honor Your Word, God, by believing You have made me a new creation in Christ.)

Observe it!
Hear and attend to what you learned from this chapter. Take a closer look, thoroughly examine what the Bible uncovers about God's ability, plans and purpose, Jesus' nature, or your identity. Do a word study, a character study. Is there more to uncover? Get curious!

Live it!
Choose to conform to your new identity by living it out.

Depend on it!
Is there anything that was uncovered in this chapter that seems impossible and yet is promised? Write out the promise and memorize it.

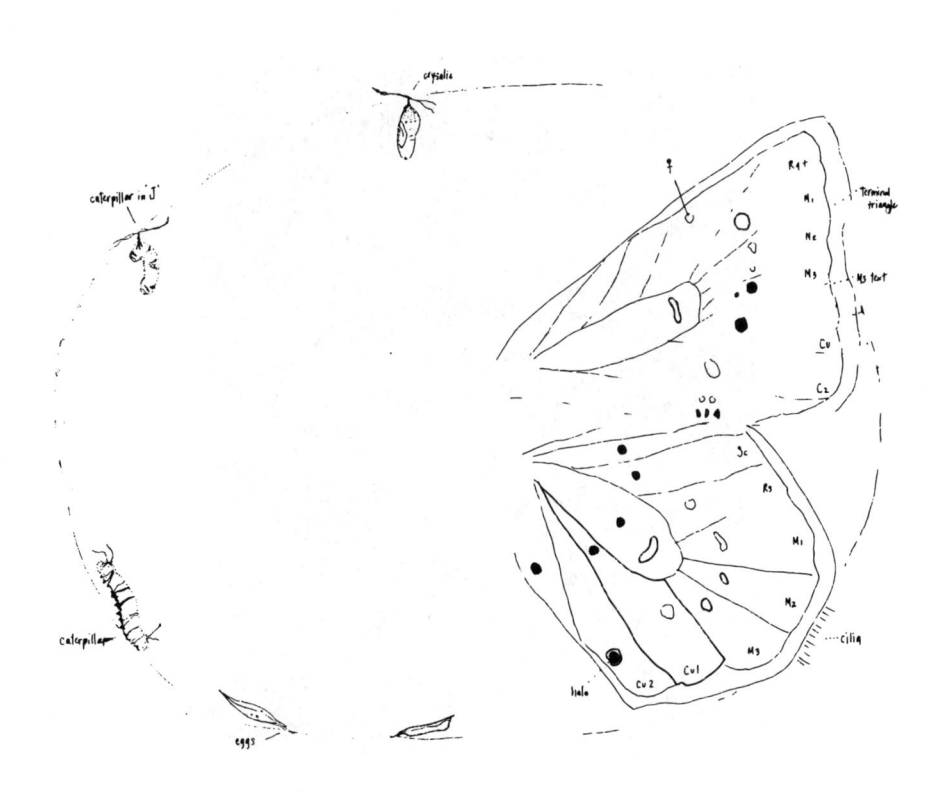

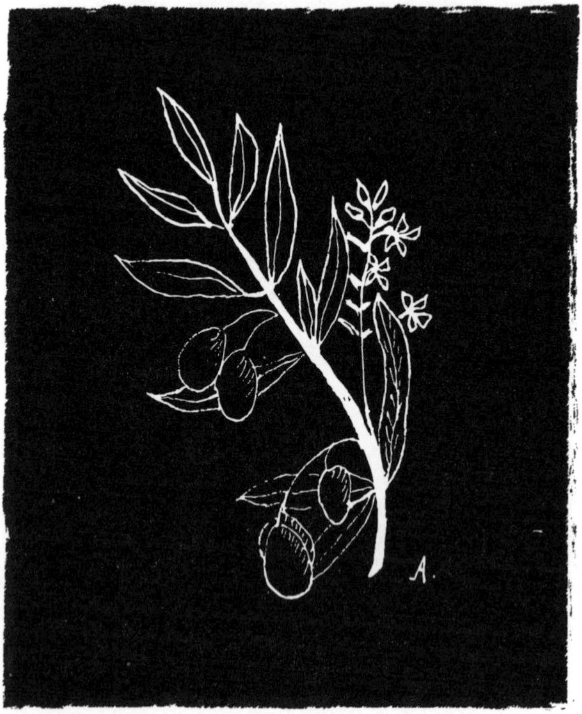
A.

chapter 14

I AM A FRUIT BEARER

I am the vine, you are the branches. He who abides in Me, and I in him, bears much fruit; for without Me you can do nothing... By this My Father is glorified, that you bear much fruit; so you will be My disciples.
John 15:5, 8

Jesus is the creator and giver of life. He makes new life from His. We are never more like Jesus, reflecting and imaging His beauty, than when our lives are bearing fresh life-giving fruit. And it is a miraculous birthing! By virtue of being grafted into Jesus, trusting and resting in Him, our lives will bear living spiritual fruit.

1. Read John 14:16–20.
   Record what you learn about being "in Christ."

2. Read Romans 11:16–20.
   By what means are we grafted into Jesus?

3. Read John 15:1–16.
   a. Who are we grafted into? Who tends to this life in Christ? (verse 1)

   b. How do we abide in Jesus?

   c. How do we abide in His love? (verse 10)

d. What has Jesus appointed that we should do? (verse 16)

e. How do we bear fruit?

f. How is more fruit born? (verses 2 and 5)

g. How is God glorified in our lives? (verse 8)

h. What words does Jesus use to describe our relationship to Him as a fruit bearer?
Verses 2 and 5

Verse 8

Verses 14–15

i. What does Jesus say will remain in us as we remain in Him? (verse 11)

j. How does Jesus describe great love? (Verse 13)

The Greek word for *abide* is *meno*. It means "to remain, continue to be present, to remain as one, not to become another or different." Our pride wants to fashion and form an identity of its own, we want to be seen as unique, someone who stands out or stands apart. As we remain in Christ, attentive to our attachment, we will conform to our new nature and will be kept from going rogue like a wild olive shoot. He adopts us, grafts us into Himself, our old wild nature roots are broken off, and we are fused to His nature. Our veins begin to fill and flow with His love, truth and power. Our very nature is transformed and this new life we now live begins to bear fresh fruit.

We are grafted into Jesus by God through faith. Now, life-giving spiritual energy is flowing to us and through us!

4. Considering the full definition of the word *abide* and the fact that we have already been grafted into Him, why do you think Jesus tells us to abide in Him?

5. In your own words describe what it means to abide in Christ.

6. In what three things does Jesus tell us to abide? (John 15)

   a. Verses 4–5

   b. Verse 7

   c. Verse 9

ABIDING IN HIS PRESENCE

7. Record what you learn about God's Holy Spirit living in you.

   a. John 14:17

   b. Romans 8:9–11

   c. Colossians 1:27

Circle the statements you sometimes believe or do. Look up the verses attached to the statements you circled. Choose a verse to write out and memorize.

The Holy Spirit is not in me.
(John 14:17)

I ignore the Holy Spirit.
(Romans 8:12–13; Ephesians 4:30)

I doubt that God can bear fruit from my life.
(John 15:4–5)

I am sometimes separate from God.
(John 14:16; Romans 8:38)

I can be separated from God.
(Matthew 28:20; Hebrews 13:5)

8. How might doubting that God has given you His Holy Spirit to live in you restrict fruit bearing?

9. What are the results of ignoring the presence of the Holy Spirit?

   a. What helps you to remain aware of the presence of the Holy Spirit in you?

ABIDING IN HIS WORD

11. Read Mark 4:1–20 And record what you learn about receiving God's Word.

Circle the statements you sometimes believe or do. Look up the verses attached to the statements you circled. Choose a verse to write out and memorize.

Some of God's Word is not true.
(Psalm 18:30; 119:160; Proverbs 30:5; John 1:17)

Some of God's Word is not relevant.
(Romans 15:4; 1 Thessalonians 2:13; 2 Timothy 3:15)

Some of God's Word is not realistic.
(2 Timothy 3:16; 2 Peter 1:20–21)

The Bible is not accurate.
(2 Timothy 3:16; 2 Peter 1:19–21)

I doubt that some promises are really possible.
(2 Corinthians 1:20)

God's Word is not a necessary part of my everyday life.
(Psalm 119:98; 2 Timothy 3:15)

God's Word is not living.
(Hebrews 4:12)

12. How would believing any of the previous statements possibly undermine your identity as a fruit bearer in Christ?

ABIDING IN HIS LOVE

13. Read the following verses and record what you learn about abiding in God's love.
    a. Romans 5:5

    b. Ephesians 3:14–21

    c. 1 John 4:16

To be *rooted and grounded* is a term used to describe a plant that is exposed to wind, storm or shaking so that the roots are stimulated to strike down, putting energy into root strengthening and growth in order to firmly fix and establish the vigorous health of the plant.

Circle the statements you sometimes believe or do and look up the verses attached to the statements you circled. Choose a verse to write out and memorize.

My sin has separated me from the love of God.
(Romans 8:39)

God's love for me is dependent upon my worthiness.
(Romans 5:8)

I cannot love the way God loves.
(1 John 4:17, 19)

There are some people that God would not want me to love.
(Mathew 5:44; 22:37–39; 1 John 3:11; 4:11, 21)

14. How would believing any of the previous statements eat away at your identity as a fruit bearer in Christ?

15. What quality does Jesus attach to the fruit He has chosen and appointed us to go and bear (John 15:16)

16. Read 1 Corinthians 13:13.
   a. What are we told will endure the test of time?

b. What is the significance of your life bearing enduring fruit?

17. Why do you think it is important to know and believe that part of your identity in Christ is a fruit bearer?

God's glory is connected with the fruit attached to our spiritual life. Our cooperation with the Vinedresser, the cultivating of our identification with and attachment to Jesus, our awareness of the Holy Spirit are places the enemy is hacking at and trying to destroy. Satan wants to minimize the glory of God born from a life that is attached to His Son. Our temptation is to look at ourselves instead of looking at God to do what only He can do in and through a life bound to His. These roots connected with your identity must be secured, guarded and established. When you are firmly rooted and grounded in Christ the sap of God's divine love and power can flow vigorously free. It is then the purpose of God for your life, bringing glory to Him, will be fulfilled with a joyful abandonment of the self-life.

Your identity in Christ is bountiful with purpose!

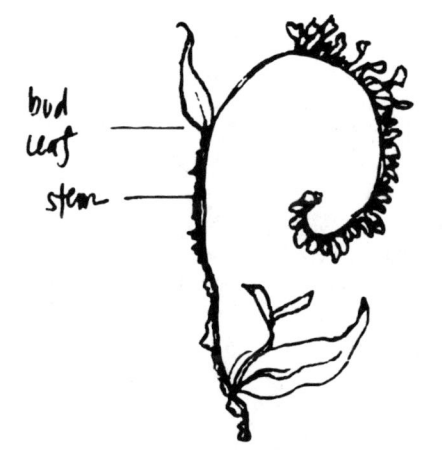

Behold...
He shall be like a tree
Planted by the rivers of water,
That brings forth its fruit in its season,
Whose leaf also shall not wither;
And whatever he does shall prosper.
Psalm 1:3

Believe it!
Was something uncovered about your identity in this chapter that is challenging your faith?

Enjoy it!
What did you behold about your identity in this chapter that has you excited?

Honor it!
Make a decision to honor God by choosing to believe what He says about who you are in Christ. Write your declaration: (i.e., I choose to honor Your Word, God, by believing You have made me a new creation in Christ.)

Observe it!
Hear and attend to what you learned from this chapter. Take a closer look, thoroughly examine what the Bible uncovers about God's ability, plans and purpose, Jesus' nature, or your identity. Do a word study, a character study. Is there more to uncover? Get curious!

Live it!
Choose to conform to your new identity by living it out.

Depend on it!
Is there anything that was uncovered in this chapter that seems impossible and yet is promised? Write out the promise and memorize it.

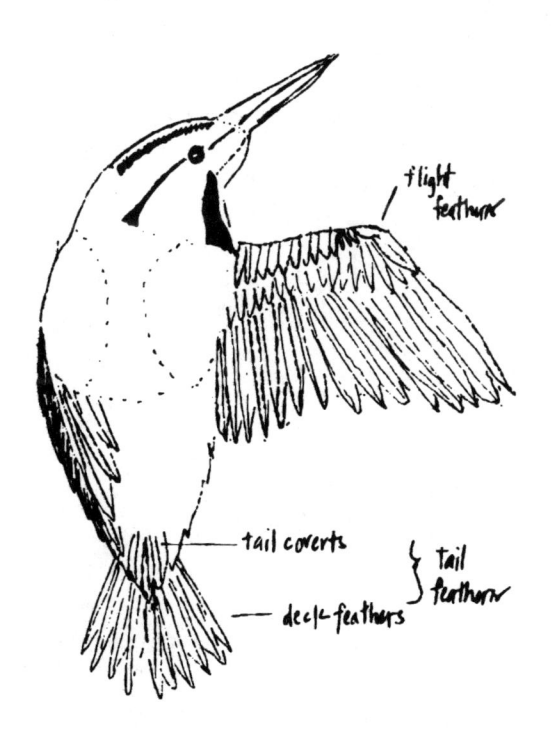

Olea Europaea L.

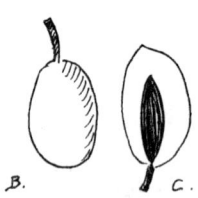

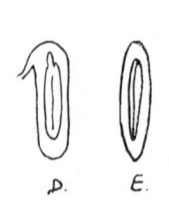

A. Habitus
B. Fr.
C. Fr. mit durch
D. U
E. S
F. Bl

chapter 15

I AM AN AMBASSADOR

Now all things are of God, who has reconciled us to Himself through Jesus Christ, and has given us the ministry of reconciliation, that is, that God was in Christ reconciling the world to Himself, not imputing their trespasses to them, and has committed to us the word of reconciliation. Now then, we are ambassadors for Christ, as though God were pleading through us: we implore you on Christ's behalf, be reconciled to God. For God made Him who knew no sin to be sin for us, that we might become the righteousness of God in Him.
2 Corinthians 5:18-21

Living in the reality of who we are in Christ is far-reaching, not only edifying ourselves but becoming a potential benefit to everyone and everything we come into contact with. When we live out our identity in Christ we are set free from creating our own identity and from striving to project that identity to the world around us. We are free to reflect and represent the life of Christ in us and we are released into the ministry of our King. God has made us His ambassadors in Christ, called to represent Him here on earth. This will require a heart that is loyal to Him. Being united to Jesus means there should no longer be a distinction between my heart and His heart, my plans and His plans, my way and His way. God's Spirit is at work bringing all that we think and pursue into alignment with Him.

1. What is an ambassador?

2. Use 2 Corinthians 5:18–21 to answer the following questions.
    a. Who has authorized you to represent God?

    b. What service has God given to you? (verses 18 and 20)

c. What does *reconciled to God* mean? (You can use a dictionary, concordance, 2 Corinthians 5:18–21 and Colossians 1:19–22 to help you formulate an answer).

d. What is the word of reconciliation appointed to us by God?

3. Read Romans 5:1, 10–11 and Ephesians 2:13–14 to describe how someone is reconciled to God.

There is so much to the idea of being ambassadors! An ambassador does not speak to please his audience, but the King who sent him. An ambassador does not speak on his own authority; his own opinions or demands mean little. He simply says what he has been commissioned to say. But an ambassador is more than a messenger; he is also a representative, and the honor and reputation of his country are in his hands.
David Guzik

When God saved you, He transferred you from living under the tyrannical and dark rulership of Satan into the Kingdom of God's Son, a Kingdom of light. He changed our citizenship.

   4. Record what you discover from the following verses concerning your citizenship:
      a. Philippians 3:20

      b. Hebrews 11:13–16

You are no longer identified as a citizen of earth, your new identity in Christ is a citizen of heaven. Now you live on earth as a foreigner and a pilgrim.

   5. What King and country have you been assigned to represent

   6. What foreign land has God assigned and sent you to be His ambassador?

   7. What mindset and qualities, displayed in the rugged lives described in Hebrews 11, would be beneficial to adopt in order to live in your identity as a citizen of heaven and ambassador of God?

8. Describe how your life is representing the truth of your identity as a citizen of heaven and foreigner on earth.

We have been made in God's image, born again by the Spirit of God and given the divine nature of Jesus. We don't have to try to imitate His nature, we simply live in His nature and He will shine. We do, however, have a free will to choose who's heart and mind we will represent.

9. What part do you think loyalty has in the life of an ambassador?

10. Take some time to prayerfully examine your loyalty to representing God as His ambassador in these aspects of your life. Take note next to any areas that need to be aligned with God's plans and purpose.

    Time

    Attitude

    Conversation

    Resources

    Energy

    Attention

Pursuits

Passions/Interests

Dreams/Goals

For it is God who works in you to will and to act on behalf of His good pleasure. Philippians 2:13 Berean Study Bible

11. Look again at 2 Corinthians 5:20.
    a. Describe the passion and intensity Paul used to communicate the word of reconciliation as God's ambassador to the Corinthians.

    b. Why do you think Paul was such a passionate ambassador?

    c. How passionate do you believe God is about being reconciled with humanity?

    d. Do you share God's intensity about reconciliation?

*The love of Christ had pressed Paul's energies
into one force, turned them into one channel,
and then driven them forward with a wonderful
force, till he and his fellows had become a mighty
power for good, ever active and energetic.*
Spurgeon

What a high and holy calling we have been given by God! He has committed to His children the sacred work of representing Him to the world. Apprehending our identity as God's ambassador will activate and propel us into a new and glorious life of freedom in Christ. Living as His ambassador will cut the ties of loyalty to our old identity as a citizen of earth. We can be free to be a living representation of Jesus Christ.

*We are one with Jesus, He in us and we in Him.
He is the head, and as members of His body,
we are the living, breathing expression of Christ
on earth. We may grieve at how far short of this
identity we fall, but it's still our true identity.
Our representation (as ambassadors of God)
isn't simply honorary, ceremonial, or theoretical.
It's real. He is actually living within us. He guides
our wills, desires, words, actions, relationships,
circumstances, and steps according to the power
of His Spirit at work within us. Our relationship
with Him is beyond one-to-one; it's simply one—
He and us in union with each other. And the more
we believe that, the more we will
experience it each day.*
*The One Year Heaven on Earth Devotional: 365
Daily Invitations to Experience
God's Kingdom Here and Now
by Chris Tiegreen, Walk Thru the Bible*

BEHOLD

> Behold...
> So Jesus said to them again, "Peace to you!
> As the Father has sent Me, I also send you."
> John 20:21

Believe it!
Was something uncovered about your identity in this chapter that is challenging your faith?

Enjoy it!
What did you behold about your identity in this chapter that has you excited?

Honor it!
Make a decision to honor God by choosing to believe what He says about who you are in Christ. Write your declaration: (i.e., I choose to honor Your Word, God, by believing You have made me a new creation in Christ.)

Observe it!
Hear and attend to what you learned from this chapter. Take a closer look, thoroughly examine what the Bible uncovers about God's ability, plans and purpose, Jesus' nature, or your identity. Do a word study, a character study. Is there more to uncover? Get curious!

Live it!
Choose to conform to your new identity by living it out.

Depend on it!
Is there anything that was uncovered in this chapter that seems impossible and yet is promised? Write out the promise and memorize it.

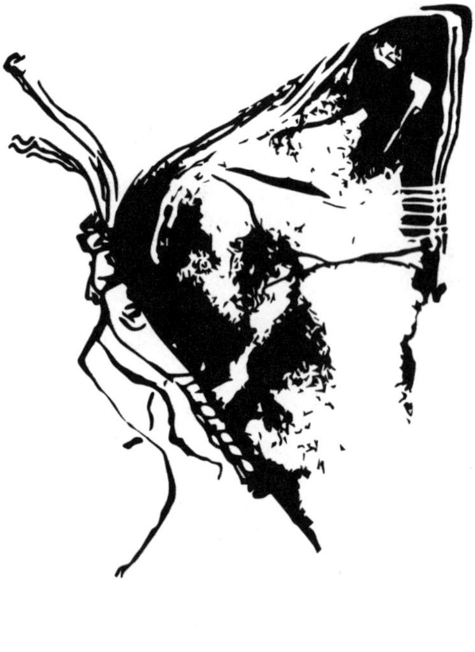

chapter 16

IDENTIFIED

Once you had no identity as a people; now you are God's people. Once you received no mercy; now you have received God's mercy.
1 Peter 2:10

Our identity includes both form and function. God originally formed man in the likeness and manner of Himself. His original purpose for man was to relate to Him in perfect union, to relate to others as He does and to relate to His creation by caring for it.

The challenge set before us in this study was to discover our true identity in Christ and to believe it.

We are children of God and saints. Not because of our good deeds or good behavior, not because we are members of a church or have made a pledge to be faithful. We are children of God and saints because it was God's good pleasure to make us so. He planned for it before the foundations of the earth. We were on His heart and mind forever. We were set apart for His plans and purpose long ago. There is nothing we can do to earn these privileges, we can only receive them and believe them by faith. And we remain children and saints no matter how rebellious and unsaintly we behave. Our behavior is a reflection of who we believe we are. If we truly believe we are loved, accepted and set apart for God our lives will reflect it. We have the Spirit working inside us helping us to believe. Before we placed our faith in Jesus our lives were stuck in patterns and habits of bad behavior that were motivated by our emptiness, loneliness, need for acceptance and unconditional love. We may not have made the connection between our behavior and being alienated from God, but it was at the root of it all. Now, we who were once far away from God have been brought near to enjoy the relationship we were designed to have with Him.

Believing we are who God says we are, places our identity on the solid ground of God's Word; it will illuminate the form and function of our identity. We will not be standing on the shaky ground of self-confidence. We will be released from trying to function in a faulty self-sufficiency mode. Now we are free to love and serve God, to love and esteem others as more important than ourselves.

The Spirit of God is helping you to agree to conform to your new nature. Will you choose to live in harmony with your new nature, or will you choose to reject it and live as you please? Rebellion against the indwelling life of Christ will feel like discord. It is conflict in the soul, a mini-coup. The Holy Spirit will contend with you until your will agrees that conforming to the nature of Christ and the image of God is the most authentic way to live.

Are you ready to be fully identified with Jesus?

1. Romans 12:2 gives us some insight into how we can cooperate with God's Spirit. Comment on the elements of the verse.

    a. Do not be conformed to this world

    b. But be transformed

    c. By the renewing

    d. Of your mind

It is that "thinking" place in us, the place of decision making that is being renewed. We simply agree to let God transform us by allowing Him to change our mind. This will always feel like a victory because it is!

2. In what ways are you struggling to agree to conform to your identity in Christ?

3. What thoughts about your identity have been renewed through this study?

   a. Are there parts of your identity that still need the convincing of the Holy Spirit for you to agree with God that you are who He says you are? If so, what are you doubting about your identity?

He has the power to bring everything under his control. By his power he will change our earthly bodies. They will become like his glorious body.
Philippians 3:21

5. Record what you discover about the identity of the church.

a. 1 Corinthians 12:7

b. Ephesians 5:25–27

c. 1 Peter 2:9

d. Revelation 19:7–9

6. Have you ever felt the temptation to not be identified with God's church? Why?

7. Why is it important to recognize that part of your identity in Christ is as a part of His body?

8. Why would it be impossible for you to identify with Christ but not identify with His church?

9. In what ways do you think the church as a whole would benefit from knowing and believing her identity in Christ?

A person living in full confidence of who they are in Christ will have a tremendous impact for good in this world. The life of Christ will be expanding in them and through them. Likewise, the church, when she takes on her identity as the bride of Christ, will be seen as the creature of strength and beauty that she is. We are people made whole and holy, co-heirs with Christ, filled with purpose and furnished with everything needed to fulfill that purpose, set free and let loose to turn the world upside down!

> *But we all, with unveiled face, beholding as in a mirror the glory of the Lord, are being transformed into the same image from glory to glory, just as by the Spirit of the Lord.*
> 2 Corinthians 3:18

Believe it!
Was something uncovered about your identity in this chapter that is challenging your faith?

Enjoy it!
What did you behold about your identity in this chapter that has you excited?

Honor it!
Make a decision to honor God by choosing to believe what He says about who you are in Christ. Write your declaration: (i.e., I choose to honor Your Word, God, by believing You have made me a new creation in Christ.)

Observe it!
Hear and attend to what you learned from this chapter. Take a closer look, thoroughly examine what the Bible uncovers about God's ability, plans and purpose, Jesus' nature, or your identity. Do a word study, a character study. Is there more to uncover? Get curious!

Live it!
Choose to conform to your new identity by living it out.

Depend on it!
Is there anything that was uncovered in this chapter that seems impossible and yet is promised? Write out the promise and memorize it.

FLYING ARROW ministries
FLYINGARROWMINISTRIES.COM

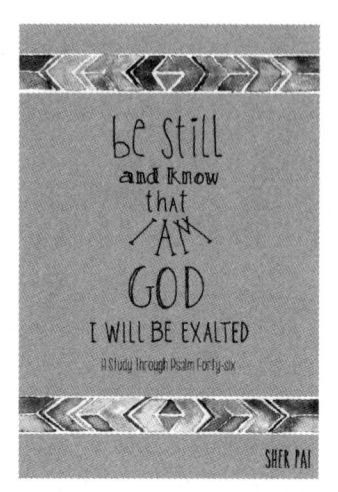

Be Still and know that I Am God. A 7 week study through Psalm 46. Also available in Spanish

Gifted for Service is an 8 week Bible study aimed at helping you discover your spiritual gifts. Also available in Spanish.

Partners in Grace is a 15 week Bible study through the book of Philippians.

Cultivating a Quiet Heart is a reflective and responsive journal created to compliment the Be Still Bible study.